GOLF, AS IT WAS IN THE BEGINNING
THE LEGENDARY BRITISH OPEN COURSES

GOL

THE LEGENDARY BR

IT WAS

BEGIN

BY MICHAEL

PRINCIPAL PHOTOGRAPHY

UNIVERSE

F, AS

TISH OPEN COURSES

IN THE

NING

FAY WITH

BY MICHAEL FREEMAN

PUBLISHING

First published in the United States of America in 2002
By UNIVERSE PUBLISHING
A Division of Rizzoli International Publications, Inc.
300 Park Avenue South
New York, NY 10010

Library of Congress Control Number: 2002058593
2002 2003 2004 2005 / 10 9 8 7 6 5 4 3 2 1

All photographs copyright © Michael Freeman, except the following:
© Patricia McNeilly: pages 160–161, 162, 164–165, 168–169
© Matthew Harris: pages 122–123, 124, 126–127, 128, 130–131

Design by Opto
Map illustrations © Brad Simon

Printed in Singapore

THIS BOOK IS THE ACCUMULATION OF GOLF EXPERIENCE THAT I HAVE GAINED OVER THE YEARS BY HOPPING ON AN AIRPLANE AND HEADING TO THE HOME OF GOLF, THE BRITISH ISLES.

I DEDICATE THIS BOOK TO MY FELLOW TRAVELING GOLFERS, GUYS THAT I HAVE ACCOMPANIED TO THE GREAT COURSES OF THE OPEN CHAMPIONSHIP AND TO ALL THE OTHER GREAT COURSES ACROSS THE POND. THREE PEOPLE IN PARTICULAR HAVE COME WITH ME ON MORE THAN ONE OCCASION AND THEIR COMPANY WAS WELL APPRECIATED. ONE IS MY GOOD FRIEND DR. GLEN RAPOPORT WITH WHOM I SAW ROYAL SAINT GEORGES, ROYAL CINQUE PORTS, AND PRINCES. HE DESERVES A MENTION FOR SURVIVING MY DRIVING ON THE KENT COAST. THE SECOND FELLOW IS THE EVER SMILING TERRY O'MALLEY MD OF BOSTON WITH WHOM I SHALL FOREVER ASSOCIATE WITH ROYAL PORTRUSH IN IRELAND. LASTLY, MY LOVELY SPOUSE, MONICA, WHO DASHED AROUND SCOTLAND AND ENGLAND WITH ME LAST SUMMER TO COMPLETE MY RESEARCH. I ONLY REGRET THAT THE ACCOMMODATIONS DID NOT MATCH THE VENUES.

TERENCE MAIKELS OF UNIVERSE PUBLISHING IS MY EDITOR AND HAS DONE A WONDERFUL JOB OF GETTING THIS BOOK TOGETHER.

I MUST THANK THE FOLLOWING PEOPLE FOR THEIR KINDNESS AND COOPERATION IN HELPING ME FINISH THIS BOOK. MY GREAT FRIEND, DAVID BOND, THE MAN WHO EMBODIES GOLF AT CARNOUSTIE, WHO ASSISTED ON THE FIRTH OF TAY. JAMIE PAXTON AT THE TURNBERRY RESORT, PETER MASON OF THE SAINT ANDREWS LINKS TRUST, JAMES MCGREGOR THE STARTER AND SOMETIME HISTORIAN OF THE MUSSELBURGH LINKS WERE ALL INSTRUMENTAL IN HELPING AT THEIR RESPECTIVE COURSES. THE SECRETARIES AT THE VARIOUS OPEN VENUES WERE VERY KIND TO ME AND SOME OF THE MOST INTERESTING PEOPLE I HAVE MET IN GOLF. THEY INCLUDE WILMA ERSKINE AT ROYAL PORTRUSH, MICHAEL GILYEAT AT ROYAL BIRKDALE, JAN CHANDLER AT ROYAL TROON, LYTTON GOODWIN AT ROYAL LYTHAM AND SAINT ANNES, BILL HOWIE AT PRINCES, GERALD WATTS AT ROYAL SAINT GEORGES, COLIN HAMMOND AT ROYAL CINQUE PORTS, CHRIS MOORE AT ROYAL LIVERPOOL, IAN BUNCH OF PRESTWICK, AND GROUP CAPTAIN JOHN PRIDEAUX AT MUIRFIELD.

I MUST ALSO MENTION HENRY WROTNIAK AND ELAINE SABETTA FROM SANDITZ TRAVEL, WHO SERVED ME SO PROFESSIONALLY IN MAKING ARRANGEMENTS ON MY TRAVELS.

ACKNOWLEDGMENTS

MANKIND HAS ALWAYS treasured competition. It has been the essence of our race since the very beginning of time. The competitive spirit has revealed itself over and over in the annals of history. Whether the by-play was mental or physical, the underpinnings have always been smarter, stronger, faster, more accurate, and generally better.

Competition has led to war. Competition has led to empires. Competition is that on which the human race has thrived since the first troglodyte wrestled his brother for the cave with the view.

As time has passed, the form of competitive behavior (with some notable exceptions) has become less bloody; it has become more civilized. The prize has gone away from simple survival to more mundane things. Yet, everyone who has ever competed in any contest knows that the prize is

THE POSTAGE STAMP (HOLE # 8) AT OLD TROON,
NOW ROYAL TROON

ABOVE: HENRY COTTON, THREE-TIME CHAMPION AT
MUIRFIELD, IN 1948

secondary to the satisfaction that the winner feels; we fight for the elation, the huge boost in self-esteem, and the glory in which to bask in front of the populace. The Romans had their chariot races, the French had their sword fights, and the English had their tournaments of the Knights.

It is not recorded as to the weather on that first day of the Championship in October 1860. All we know for sure is that a small group of those that considered themselves Professional Golfers gathered a few feet from Links Road in Prestwick, Scotland, near the first tee of the twelve-hole lay-out.

There had been matches recorded over the years pitting many of the well-known golfers of the era against each other. Most of these took the form of challenge matches. One noted golfer and his backers would dare to test the mettle of a local professional and would play a round at the home course of each contestant.

This day was different. Andrew Strath, Willie Park Jr., Old Tom Morris, George Brown, and others were here at Prestwick to identify the best professional of the day. Up to this particular year, it was generally assumed that Allan Robertson, the first professional at Saint Andrews, was the best golfer in Scotland. But alas Mr. Robertson was no longer with the firm; he had passed away in 1859.

So here they were, ready to do battle on the field of honor in the first organized professional championship of golf. In keeping with old tradition the contestants were competing for a Championship belt, which the host club had donated. This was very much of British tradition, in that a belt had been the prize in jousting tournaments.

Thus began the most enduring tournament in golf. It was truly golf, as it was in the beginning.

The Open Championship is the first and oldest golf championship. It has been played on the shores of Scotland, England, and Ireland for more than 140 years. During the period from 1860 to today, the Open Championship has been held on fourteen of the very finest links golf courses in the world.

Six of these courses are in England. Royal Saint Georges, Royal Cinque Ports, and Princes are side by side on the Kent Coast, which is on the East Coast of England and south of London. Royal Liverpool, Royal Birkdale, and Royal Lytham and Saint Annes are on the opposite coast toward the middle of the country. This area is known as the Lancashire coast and is to many Brits, it is the beach.

On the West Coast of Scotland, Prestwick, Royal Troon, and Turnberry can be found. On the

other coast, Musselburgh, Muirfield, Carnoustie, and the Old Course at Saint Andrews are located. The one remaining venue is the Royal Portrush Golf Club situated on the North Sea on the northern tip of Ireland.

The golf courses and the sea are intertwined in the story of the Open Championship. All but one of the courses directly abuts the water, this one exception being Royal Lytham and Saint Annes, which is about two blocks from the Irish Sea. So, just as man allegedly rose from the sea, competitive golf did as well.

The subject of the Open Championship is voluminous. It could well fill an entire encyclopedia. In the interest of brevity, I will attempt to convey the flavor of these fourteen fine layouts, review some of the more significant champions and highlight a few of the more stirring competitions.

With the assist of the photographs of Michael Freeman, I will walk you through some of the holes from the different venues. I chose these holes in an attempt to represent the differing challenges that have faced the contestants in the past present and future.

Let us now walk down the fairways of the Open Championship. . . .

THE ARCHITECTS The courses of the Open Championship are relatively few given the period of time that has expired since the beginning. In fact there have only been fourteen venues for the Open Championship in the 141 years that have come and gone since the first shot was hit at Prestwick in

1860.

The courses employed have origins that are ancient by golfing standards. Most of the clubs were established in the nineteenth century, although some of them go back even further. Two of the courses were built for the same club, the Honourable Company of Edinburgh Golfers. Those are Old Musselburgh and Muirfield. The latter replaced the Musselburgh golf course around the turn of the past century.

The oldest course is, by no surprise, the Royal and Ancient at Saint Andrews. Its origins are shrouded in mystery; in fact it is suggested that it appeared naturally. Alistar MacKenzie, the renowned British architect, suggested that Saint Andrews differs from all other golf courses in that it has always been deemed a sacrilege to interfere with its natural beauties, and thereby it has been left untouched for centuries. Research tells us, however, that the course evolved over a period of four centuries and was made an eighteen-hole course sometime around 1860. Credit for its present day design is given to Allan Robertson, Old Tom Morris, James Braid, John Stutt, as well as Alistar MacKenzie. The general feeling has always been, though, that none of the above-mentioned was more than revisionists of

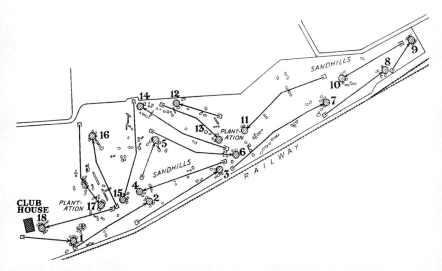

little impact and that the Old Course has really remained a work of nature.

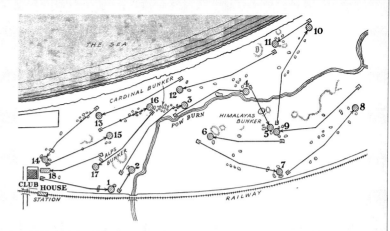

ABOVE: PRESTWICK LAYOUT IN 1924
OPPOSITE PAGE: ROYAL LYTHAM AND SAINT ANNES

The remaining courses employed through time as venues of the Open Championship owe their characters to just a handful of golf architects. Muirfield and Carnoustie were largely the work of Old Tom Morris, although Willie Park Jr., John Stutt, and James Braid made later alterations. Harry Colt, a onetime partner of MacKenzie, is credited with the original design of the Dunluce course at Portrush and practiced his handiwork at no less than four other venues (Hoylake, Royal Lytham and Saint Annes, Royal Saint Georges, and Muirfield). George Lowe Jr. was the original designer of Royal Birkdale and Royal Lytham and Saint Annes, both of which were refined by three members of the Hawtree family Charles, Frederic George, and Frederic William.

As you can see, the number of architects is quite small, yet the cumulative reputations of those that were employed are yeoman. All of the designers were well acquainted with links golf and the effects of the wind as it blew off the water. They understood the value of playing the game close to the ground, allowing for a well-struck shot to run to the hole rather than to rely on a shot hit through the air.

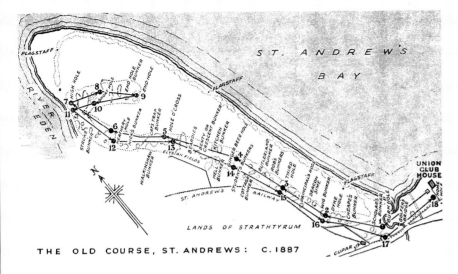

THE OLD COURSE, ST. ANDREWS: C. 1887

ABOVE: THE OLD COURSE AT SAINT ANDREWS, CIRCA 1887
OPPOSITE PAGE: ROYAL SAINT GEORGES AT TURN OF THE CENTURY

There are few, if any, trees on any of these courses. Trees can rarely survive the winds that are experienced on these links. With the exception of small streams, known as burns, there are little or no internal water hazards on these courses. This leaves only two other hazards to contend with, bunkers and rough.

Bunkers are plain and simple penal on all of these courses. They have been placed in exactly those spots that will be found by a well-struck shot that is hit slightly off line. More often than not, when the player finds a fairway bunker, the penalty is severe. Rather than playing forward to the hole, he must find the closest egress and swallow his pride.

Nature provides the rough. It is not the three-inch variety of Kentucky bluegrass that players from the States are so familiar with. It is not even the severe six-inch draconian rough that the United States Golf Association offers at their Major Championships. No it is far more hellish than we ever see in the States. It is composed of bracken, whins, gorse, and heather. Rather than explaining each of these devilish plants in detail, suffice to say that often one is relieved that their ball is lost allowing a fresh start instead of having to confront these hounds of nature.

All of the architects that created the Open venues understood the elements, the natural flora and the game of golf. That is why today courses that were created as long ago as 140 years are still as relevant as at the time of their creation.

THE GREAT ONES Every great golfer has played in the Open Championship. For the first sixty or so if its existence, the Open Championship was the most coveted award in all of golf. In the 1920s the popularity of the game in the United States, along with incumbent press that was afforded the Professional Golf Association and its tournaments, probably pushed the relatively infant (established in 1896) U. S. Open ahead in importance. Of course, the importance is relative. Although the U. S. Open have superseded the Open Championship in America, most of the rest of the world still believed that the Open Championship was still the top dog.

From the beginning, the best players in the British Isles competed annually for the crown. No one family was singularly as successful at capturing it as the father-son duo of Old Tom Morris and Young Tom Morris. Old

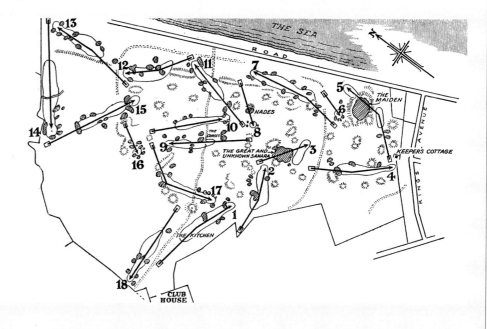

Tom was the first multiple winner in 1861 and 1862 and followed with victories in 1864 and 1867. Young Tom took over where the old man left off by capturing the belt in 1868, 1869, and 1970. With his victory in 1870, Young Tom Morris actually retired the Championship Belt. The understanding from the onset of the first Open Championship was that any man who won the belt three years in a row would get to keep it. This posed a bit of a problem in 1871, as there was no longer a prize for the winner. The Open Championship was not held that year, due to this complication. By 1872, three Clubs, Prestwick, the Royal and Ancient, and Musselburgh, shared the cost of a new trophy when the Claret Jug was purchased for thirty pounds sterling. The first name inscribed on the jug is that of Young Tom Morris, making him the only participant to take the Championship in four successive outings. The dominance of the Open Championship by the Morris family of Saint Andrews ended in 1872.

Young Tom failed to defend in 1873, instead finishing in third place. In 1874 Young Tom was the runner up in his final attempt. By Christmas of 1874, he died at the tender age of twenty-four.

In 1894, John Henry Taylor of Devon, England, kicked off another era of repeat winners. Taylor, along with Harry Vardon, who hailed from the Channel Islands, and James Braid of Fife, Scotland, monopolized the engraving on the Claret Jug. In the next twenty-one years, Braid and Taylor claimed the Championship five times each. Vardon, not to be out-done, won the tournament an unparalleled six times. During this same period, this "Great Triumvirate" racked up a total of fifteen runner-up finishes. At Saint Andrews in 1900 and again at Muirfield in 1901, these masters of the game finished one, two, and three.

ABOVE: BOBBY JONES CHATTING WITH FAMOUS BRITISH AMATEUR ROGER WUTHERED AT SAINT ANDREWS IN 1927

It is ironic that while the Open Championship was waning in stature among Americans in the early 1920s, American-born golfers were making their way in greater numbers to play in the world's oldest contest. The Open Championship was won for the first time by a golfer born in the States when Walter Hagen emerged the Champion in 1922. "The Haig" followed with victories in 1924, 1928, and 1929. With his flamboyant style, Hagen revitalized the Open Championship in the eyes of Americans. For example, as Professional Golfers were not allowed access to the clubhouses of the

ABOVE: JAMES BRAID, ONE OF THE GREAT TRIUMVIRATE
AND THE ARCHITECT OF MANY OF THE OPEN COURSES
OPPOSITE PAGE: J. H. TAYLOR

host venues and made to take their meals in the kitchen, Hagen took to renting a Rolls Royce, parking it in front of the clubhouse, changing his shoes, and eating picnic lunches in the vehicle.

Walter Hagen was a great champion, but this was the era of Robert Tyre Jones Jr. Bobby won the Open Championship in 1926 at Royal Lytham and Saint Annes and at Saint Andrews in 1927. He gained the first leg of the Grand Slam in 1930 at Royal Liverpool.

Englishman Henry Cotton was the next to dominate, winning the Championship in 1934 at Royal St. Georges, 1937 at Carnoustie, and again after World War II in 1947 at Muirfield.

The late 1940s and the entire 1950s belonged to two players who are often forgotten in golf lore. The oversized South African Bobby Locke, still regarded by some as the greatest putter of all times, sparred repeatedly with Australian Peter Thompson for the title. Locke won in 1949 at Saint Georges, 1950 at Royal Troon, 1952 at Lytham and Saint Annes, and 1957 at the Old Course. Thompson triumphed three years in a row: 1954 at Birkdale, 1955 at Saint Andrews, and 1956 at Hoylake. The first Australian champion added yet another victory at Lytham in 1958. Eight championships in one decade was indeed a great feat for these two combatants, especially considering the difficulty of travel at the time.

A GOLFER'S STROLL THR

OUGH 18 PERFECT HOLES

THE FIRST HOLE PRESTWICK NUMBER 1

"A man is less likely to be contradicted in lauding Prestwick than
of signing the praises of any other course in Christendom." Bernard Darwin

PRESTWICK, ENGLAND • 1851
346 YARDS • PAR 4

PRESTWICK IN 1860 was a twelve-hole golf course. The Club Professional and Greenkeeper was a fellow named Tom Morris. Tom originally came from Saint Andrews, where he was an assistant to Allan Robertson. Morris and Robertson had a falling out about the use of the gutta percha golf ball, which had been invented a few years earlier. At the time of Robertson and Morris, a good portion of a professional's income was derived from boiling a top hat full of goose feathers and cramming them into a form that was sewn from either horsehide or cowhide. The featherie golf ball was the mainstay of the game. The featherie was also fragile and prone to exploding when wet. Anyhow, Robertson was the boss and so Morris moved on.

After the death of Allan Robertson, Prestwick and Morris promoted the idea of a Professional

BEYOND THE WALL IS THE ROUTE TO TRIPLE BOGEY

Championship. The Prestwick Club bought the jeweled belt and the fight was on.

Prestwick lies on the West Coast of Scotland about thirty miles west of Glasgow. It borders directly on the Irish Sea. The weather in this part of the country can be glorious, but is more often demonic. The winds that come from the Irish Sea are devastating, so ferocious that flying into the Prestwick Airport is one of the most-feared trips in the world. The golf gods, in order to make the player feel that he has been abandoned, often mix rain, wind, and cold. But, such is life. Prestwick remains a center court attraction for true golfers to this day.

There have been twenty-four Open Championships played at Prestwick. The first sixteen of these were played on the old twelve-hole layout. Six more holes were added in 1886 to bring the course to the standard, which we know today. This course was played eight more times through 1925; the Open has not returned to Prestwick since. Because of the requirement for length that is so important in holding Professional Championships today, Prestwick will probably never see another Open. The 2001 British Amateur was held there and the course received nearly unanimous accolades from the competitors, but at 6,544 yards, the course simply is not long enough for professional play.

LEFT: PRESTWICK HOLE NUMBER 1
OPPOSITE PAGE: FIRST HOLE OF THE OPEN CHAMPIONSHIP COMMEMORATIVE STONE

The champions at Prestwick were some of the giants of the game. Tom Morris Sr. (four times), Willie Park Sr. (four times), Tom Morris Jr. (four times), and Harry Vardon (three times) all took the crown at the old venue. It is interesting that these four would account for more than sixty percent of all the champions crowned here. Prestwick, then as it is today, is a course that requires imagination and a good memory. There are a number of truly blind shots. The terrain is craggy and difficult, making the placement of the drive a very important part of the quotient.

The original first hole at Prestwick was a real bear of a starter. The tee, which is memorialized today with a stone, is but a few steps off of Golf Road. The green stood some 576 yards to the east. That green today serves as the fifteenth green. In 1860 the Prestwick Club depended on natural mowing for maintenance on the course. The grass, fairway and rough, was kept in check by a fairly large herd of sheep.

THE MODERN FIRST HOLE It is difficult to think of a hole that was designed in 1886 as a modern hole, but this is indeed the case. It replaced a hole that had been in play for more than a quarter century. The hole was created to help expand the course to the new standard of eighteen holes. Tom Morris Sr., who laid out the original twelve holes in 1851 moved the tee some 100 yards south and created a hole that has an imposing

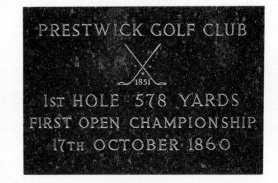

hazard off the tee. The entire hole runs parallel to the railway with little or no room for error to the right. There is a generous fairway to the left that is bordered by mounds, gorse, whins, and bunkers. The fairway shrinks dramatically about 225 yards from the tee, leaving a passage no more than 15–20 yards wide through the green.

The choice of weapon off the first tee is crucial. If one is to hit a driver, peril abounds. The railway encroaches right, the rough and the junk is left. The risk/reward is nil. This leaves the choice of either a lofted wood or a low iron. These seem like fairly conservative and reasonable options. The problem is that most players tend to push or cut both of these clubs to the right, especially when they are not warmed up. Did I mention there is no range at Prestwick?

If the player has attained position in the fairway at least 200 yards from the tee, the hole becomes much easier to handle. Less than 200 yards from the tee and the difficulty increases dramatically. The green is not big and is not totally visible from the fairway. If the approach shot is hit short, it will find a bunker. If the approach shot is long or left, the green slopes away on the chip shot. If the player drifts too far to the right, he has taken a ride on the triple bogey express.

OPPOSITE PAGE: THE PENAL NATURE OF BUNKERING IS A RECURRING THEME IN OPEN CHAMPIONSHIP GOLF. ABOVE: A VIEW FROM THE SIDE OF THE ORIGINAL PRESTWICK CLUBHOUSE

At 346 yards, one might postulate that this hole is just a friendly handshake. Those who have played it know that there is a joy buzzer in there.

THE ROYAL AND ANCIENT AT
SAINT ANDREWS   SAINT ANDREWS   NUMBER 2

BUNKERS OF THIS ILK ARE TEASERS, THEY TEMPT THE
PLAYER TO BE AGGRESSIVE WHILE THE ONLY EGRESS IS
OFTEN SIDEWAYS OR BACKWARD.

"You have to play the course [at Saint Andrews] a couple of times to understand it, as it was designed by geniuses, but I can tell you one or two things: drive carefully, and as a general rule, favour the left side of the fairways." Gary Player

NUMBER

2

SAINT ANDREWS, ENGLAND • CIRCA 1400
411 YARDS • PAR 4

IF THERE IS A magical kingdom in golf, it must be the Kingdom of Fife. In 1552, golf was played on the tip of the Firth of Fife in the town of Saint Andrews.

The Old Course of St. Andrews has acted as the stage for Scottish golfers for at least three centuries. What evolved by the 1760s was an odd yet eclectic collection of twelve greens, which represented the twenty-two holes on the links. In actuality there were really forty-four holes because the course could be played backward as well as forward. In 1764, it was decided to abandon two of the greens and continue the play at eighteen holes. This became the standard for the number of holes on a golf course.

Since its beginnings in 1754, the Royal and Ancient Golf Club has called the Old Course home.

The stately, timeless building that stands behind the first tee is the most recognized and revered clubhouse in golf. The Royal and Ancient in 1874 adopted the rules of the game as laid out by the Honourable Company of Edinburgh Golfers and has administered them ever since. The Royal and Ancient set the standard for fair competition and, by example, the integrity with which the game is played today.

Golf differs from all other sports in that the competitor is responsible for obeying the rules. If a player commits an infraction, it is the duty of that player to penalize himself. It is an outgrowth of the respect for honesty and fair play that emanates from the Royal and Ancient that allows for this self-policing game to thrive.

THE OPENS AT SAINT ANDREWS There have been twenty-six Open championships held at the Old Course since 1879. Twenty-five of these were played on a course that very much resembles the course as it is today. In 1885, the singular exception, the course may have looked very similar to what it is today but the holes in this Championship were played in reverse. It seems that at the time, the course was played alternately, left-handed or right-handed, meaning that the loop was started to the left some weeks from the first tee to the seventeenth green and other weeks in the other direction.

No longer is the course played in this fashion, but the design is so ultimately clever, it could be with very little alteration. This is not the only oddity of the course. There are only eleven greens. The first, ninth, seventeenth, and eighteenth holes have greens of their own. All the other holes share a green with the hole whose number when added to its mate equals eighteen. So the second shares with 16, third with 15, etc. This of course makes for the largest greens on any golf course, often times leaving the player putts as long as 200 feet.

To win the Open at Saint Andrews has always been considered one of the greatest feats in golf. The ground is hallowed in the tradition of the game in the Cradle of Golf. James Braid won here twice, as did J. H. Taylor and Jack Nicklaus. Bobby Jones won the Open here only once but won the British Amateur at the Old Course in 1930 as the second leg of his journey to capture the Impregnable Quadrilateral. Snead, Ballesteros, Faldo, and John Daly won victories here.

It is no wonder why the ever history-conscious Tiger Woods came to Saint Andrews so well prepared and confident as he did in 2000. He virtually annihilated both the BELOW: THE WORLD-RENOWNED ROYAL AND ANCIENT CLUBHOUSE field and the defenses of the grand Old Course on his march to an eight-

shot victory. Tiger used his prowess as the longest and straightest driver of the golf ball in the history of the game to defeat the Links. The weather was favorable that week, allowing for lower scores, and conditions on the Old Course were perfect. Nonetheless, he won by eight

DIFFICULTY ON THE SECOND HOLE IS INCREASED DUE TO
THE LACK OF FLAT LIES AND A WIND THAT BLOWS
TOWARD THE OUT OF BOUNDS.

strokes over the best field of players ever assem-

bled. There is no doubt in this author's mind

that Mr. Woods could not conceive of any other

name being inscribed on the Claret Jug next to the year 2000.

To put the Tiger victory in historical perspective, his winning score of 269 (19 under) was sixty-one shots lower than the first seventy-two-hole Open Championship won at Saint Andrews by J. H. Taylor and forty-nine shots lower than Braid, who first used the modern golf ball in 1905. Although the Tiger really only broke the mark of Nick Faldo in 1990 by one shot, the eight-stroke margin was the largest margin of victory in modern times and tied the likes of J. H. Taylor and James Braid. Never has anyone dominated a single major Championship in the fashion that Tiger did that week.

THE KENT COAST · ROYAL CINQUE PORTS

"Golf at Deal is very good indeed—fine, straight-ahead, long-hitting golf wherein
the fives are likely to be many and the fours, few. " Bernard Darwin

NUMBER
3

DEAL, ENGLAND • 1892
494 YARDS • PAR 5

IN 55 AD, JULIUS CAESAR crossed the English Channel and landed on the Kent Coast. He liked it so

much, he came back a year later in 56. Caesar had good taste.

In the southeast corner of England, the Kent Coast is a civilized yet somewhat rugged place.

Reachable by the railway from London, it is one of the most popular areas for London-based golf

clubs. Some of the best little known golf courses are situated here. They are classic in design and very,

very private. Playing them is a pleasure; man against man, man against the course, and more than any-

thing else is man against nature. The wind is always a factor at the seaside courses in the British Isles,

but on the Kent Coast, it is a constant companion.

Three venues that have hosted the Open Championship can be found side by each on the Kent

Coast. In Sandwich, the ever-regal Royal St. Georges sits right next door to the Princes course where the 1932 Open was held. Connected by one of the shortest and most interesting toll roads anyone has ever traveled, the Royal Cinque Ports Golf Club adjoins its two siblings to the south.

Royal Cinque Ports and Royal Saint Georges were considered equals at one time in the eyes of the movers and shakers of the Open Championship. Saint Georges preceded Cinque Ports on the rotation, hosting its first Open in 1894. It was employed again in 1899 and 1904 and continues to be an Open venue to this day. Deal was first used in 1909 and was considered to be a regular hosting club. Unfortunately for Royal Cinque Ports, luck and the elements have removed it from the list. Princes suffered a different fate, the victim of being a staging area for troops during World War II and forever lost due to the trampling it took. This will be explained in a later chapter.

World War I was the first impediment for continuing Deal in the rotation, although Royal Cinque Ports was the site for the re-establishment of the world's oldest golf tournament in 1920. It would be the last hurrah for this wonderful old course. It was scheduled to be the venue for the 1938 Open but flooding on the course rendered it unusable. It was moved that year to Saint Georges. Again, it was scheduled to host in 1949 but the course had not fully recovered from the battering it took from maneuvers during World War II. Once again, Saint Georges stepped up and held the Open.

So, Royal Cinque Ports has been relegated to the history books as an Open venue. Flooding problems persist, though they do not take away from this magnificent course and the classic club that occupies the ground. The club remains a vibrant part of the Kent Coast. Managed by the always efficient Colin Hammond, the club is warm and approachable.

J. H. Taylor was the first winner at Cinque Ports taking the Championship by a margin of four strokes. In 1920, little known George Duncan overcame a deficit of thirteen strokes, following two opening rounds of eighty to capture the Claret Jug by two strokes over Sandy Herd. Both of these championships were played in the era of wooden shafted clubs. It is difficult to imagine that the professionals of the day were so skilled that they could cover the ground at a course like Cinque Ports near par.

The finish at Cinque Ports is truly a bear. After the tenth hole, there is no reprieve for even the best of players. Eleven plays 441 yards into a left to right wind. The out of bounds lurks to the right. Then comes the home stretch. Twelve, par four at 471 yards; thirteen, 420 par four; fourteen, 200-plus par three; fifteen, 417 par four; sixteen, 450-plus par four; seventeen, 375 par four; and eighteen, 420-plus par four will test the mettle of any player. The wind is steady, predictable, and hard. Velocity is rarely less than 25 MPH. It is hard to imagine that the great players of the early twentieth century could complete this course successfully with the equipment they employed.

NUMBER 3 I chose this hole because it is just plain beautiful. It is a short par five of about 475 yards. It also plays down the prevailing wind and my intent was to play it with a set of wooden shafted

THERE ARE FEW STRAIGHT OR LEVEL PUTTS ON THIS
DIABOLICAL THIRD GREEN.

clubs. When I visited the club for the first time in May 2000, I was delighted to find out that the Professional, Colin Hammond, was a wooden shaft club enthusiast. After a little discussion, I challenged him to a one-hole match for five pounds. He readily accepted, so readily that I knew I was in trouble. We ambled out to the third tee to do battle.

We employed one of the older tees that was used in the 1920 Open Championship. The fairway glistened in the distance. The driving area is quite generous, which would tend to give a player some confidence. There is not enough room for a loose swing. If the player wanders from the fairway, the prospect becomes bleak. There is essentially a straight line to the green from the tee. The ground lowers from the tee to the fairway and then raises again as one approaches the green. The playing area also narrows as the fairway nears the green. Two fairly impressive mounds stand as the Praetorian Guards short of the green discouraging a wandering play from the fairway. The green is the most impressive part of the hole. The front is considerably lower than the fairway and it raises toward the back right. Words cannot describe the putting surface. Suffice it to say, it is outright perfect.

Back to the match. We both hit solid drives down the center of the fairway some 210 yards short of the green. We faced uphill shots over the fairway bunkers to the lay-up area in front of the putting surface. I must say we both played skillful shots short of the green leaving ourselves reasonable pitch shots to the dance floor. I pitched with my niblick about twenty feet short of the pin, leaving myself a straight uphill putt. My opponent pitched to the left of the pin slightly closer than I did.

I measured the putt, picked a line and putted the ball to within six inches of the hole. My putt was graciously conceded. The Pro quickly set up to his effort and stroked it directly into the hole. I once again asked myself why I am so often the victim of a lucky putt.

Golf is golf and a bet is a bet. I tendered a five pound note in keeping with the time honored tradition that fast pay makes fast friends. I shook my opponent's hand and immediately started to figure out where this five pounds would be on my expense report to my publisher.

If you do get to the Kent Coast, something I highly recommend, do not miss Royal Cinque Ports.

GOLF IN THE
ANCIENT BURGH MUSSELBURGH

NUMBER
4

THE STONE WALL THAT ADJOINS THE LEFT OF
MRS. FORMAN'S SPELLS TROUBLE FOR THOSE
WHO OVERSHOOT.

"This grand old course is probably the best historical golfing bargain in the world.
The holes remain virtually unchanged from when the British Open was last held here in 1889
(won by Willie Park Jr.)." Robert Kroeger, *Complete Guide to the Golf Courses of Scotland*

NUMBER
4

MUSSELBURGH, ENGLAND • 1774
533 YARDS • PAR 5

THE HONOURABLE COMPANY of Edinburgh Golfers was approached by the Prestwick Golf Club in 1871 to share in the cost of a new trophy for the Open Championship. With the contribution of the Royal and Ancient, Prestwick, and the Honourable Company, a Claret Jug was purchased for thirty pounds sterling. At that time, it was decided that the Open Championship would be hosted on a rotating basis among the three clubs. In 1872, the Open returned to Prestwick; in 1873, Saint Andrews saw their first Open; in 1874 the tournament moved to Musselburgh.

Musselburgh abuts Edinburgh to the east. It stands to the inland side of the East Lothian Peninsula, which is bordered to the north by the Firth of Fourth. The Old Course was in the downtown area directly by the sea. This has since changed, in that, land has been reclaimed from the Firth

and now the course is about 200 yards from the water. The Honourable Company has moved their golfing facility east to the fabulous linksland in Gullane.

What has not changed is the non-assuming nature and charm of the Old Course. It was built in and around the confines of a racetrack. This course is the epitome of simplicity. Nine holes adorn the landscape. The holes are straightforward and without guile. There are no hidden hazards, no unseemly turns. The course stands naked in front of the player and asks only that the skill of the participant be applied in precise fashion.

When the course was employed for the six Open championships, it hosted the order of the holes, dictating that the start was actually away from the starters shed. It opened with a fairly simple par 4 of 350 yards known as The Graves. The player then faced eight more holes with names like The Table, The Bathing Coach, and The Gas. All of the holes are well designed and challenging, yet none any more so than Mrs. Forman's.

MRS. FORMAN'S One might think that Mrs. Forman's is an odd name for a golf hole and with good reason. Yet, at Musselburgh, Mrs. Forman's is a landmark second only to the links themselves.

The hole at the time of the Opens was a par 5 that emanated from the interior of the racetrack at the easternmost end. The drive is the only blind shot on the golf course, played over the rails of the track downhill to a fairly generous fairway. A drive that was hooked, pushed, or sliced caused a degree of woe in that the areas off the fairway are strewn with whins and gorse. The truly unfortunate failed to carry the surface of the racetrack and found themselves faced with the ruts, mud, and even more unpleasant detritus that can be found on your average raceway. The rules made the surface of the track part of the course, ergo the employment at the time of water irons and rut irons. There is no historical information as to which club was employed to remove the ball from horse pies.

From there, the player would lay up to a neck in front of the green. The daring golfer could have conceivably gone for the green in two but was faced with the perils of out of bounds, left, right, and long. The play from the lay-up area depended on the position of the pin on the large, undulating, and deceptive green. A ball that was put on the green in the wrong position would invariably have caused a three putt at the time. It would be equally difficult today.

Many contestants in the Open championships met with great adversity at Mrs. Forman's, yet all could soothe their bruised psyches immediately. Just a quick walk off the back of the green is the door to Mrs. Forman's, the pub that has adjoined the fourth green for more than a hundred years.

LOOKING BACK AT THE RACETRACK FROM THE GREEN

THE CHAMPIONS All of the Championships held at Musselburgh consisted
of four rounds of the nine-hole layout in one day. Mungo Park, the brother of the first Open Champion, Willie Park, won the first in 1874. Mungo was followed by Jamie Anderson in 1877, Bob Ferguson in 1880, Willie Fernie in 1883, David Brown in 1886, and Willie Park Jr. in 1889. The score of 159 posted by Mungo Park in 1874 was not bettered until David Brown shot 157 in 1886. In 1889, Willie Park Jr. scored 155 to capture the Claret Jug.

Bob Ferguson, the winner at Musselburgh in 1880 also won in 1881 and 1882. He tied Fernie at Musselburgh in 1883, but lost in a thirty-six-hole playoff.

Bob was one of the more interesting champions. This three-peat champ, nearly a four-time winner, had some advantage over the field at Musselburgh; he was a professional caddie at the course.

The champions at Musselburgh are easily forgotten with the passage of time. Well more than one

hundred years have passed since the Old Course was employed as the venue for the Championship. The names of the winners may have been forgotten but their faces have not. On the front of the Old Musselburgh clubhouse, across the street from the venerable links, are all of the champions, etched in bas-relief for all to remember.

HOW TO REACH THE BACK DOOR The best way to play Musselburgh is with the equipment of the time of the Championship. If you do not have wooden-shafted clubs, do not worry. James McGregor, the Stuart of the starting house will rent them to you.

It is a real test to see if your golfing ability will hold up if you recede in implements and play with the clubs of a different age. I did exactly this when I visited Musselburgh in August 2001.

The sight from the fourth tee is daunting. All that I could see was racetrack and trouble. The definition from the tee is not bad. It was easy to perceive the line of the hole, even though the fairway drops down from the far side of the racecourse. A well-struck shot placed me in the fairway about 215 yards from the green. From here I took dead aim with my trusty spoon and sent the orb flying into an area of the fairway left and just short of the green. This left a tricky pitch to a back left position. With a deft flip of my pitching niblick, I ascended to the green some four feet from the cup. After a firm putt entered the hole for a modern day par, my wife and I retired to Mrs. Forman's for a beverage.

To be totally honest about my par at Mrs. Forman's, I must add that the wind was aiding me and rather than a gutta percha ball, I had the Titleist Pro V in play.

EVERY HOLE A
POSTCARD ROYAL BIRKDALE

NUMBER
5

"If I had the chance to relive just one piece of golf of all that I have seen, I think it would have
to be that stretch played by Palmer in the second round in 1961 on his almost predestined way to victory."
Peter Ryde, on Arnold Palmer's 1961 Open Championship at Birkdale

NUMBER

5

SOUTHPORT, ENGLAND • 1889
344 YARDS • PAR 4

THERE IS A TRUE ART to designing golf courses among the dunes and by the sea. The creator has to find a means to meld the natural surroundings into golf holes without artificial trickery and expose to the player and the world the beauty of the site. This is an art that has escaped many of the golf architects of the world. George Low, Fred Hawtree, and J. H. Taylor were not bereft of this talent. At Royal Birkdale, they produced a challenging natural golf course as well as stunning views that are only duplicated on the finest tracts in the world.

The dunes land south of Southport on the Lancashire coast is probably one of the most advantageous pieces of property on which to build a golf course. The soil is composed of sand. The ground rolls and swells gradually allowing for minute, yet devilish, perception problems for the player.

Distances cannot be accurately judged by the eye, making the player rely on printed yardages. This is truly unsettling for the best of players. The doubt created in the mind when the printed yardage does not equal that which is perceived causes even the best of players to second guess the shots they are seeking to execute. Add a thirty-mile-an-hour wind and a little friendly shower from the sea and the guessing game further escalates.

Royal Birkdale hosted the Open Championship for the first time in 1954. In the ensuing forty-seven years, the quest for the Claret Jug has returned six times. None of these championships was more important than the 1961 Open.

LEFT: ROYAL BIRKDALE HOLE NUMBER 5

After World War II, travel to the United Kingdom was difficult and accommodations were sparse. Sam Snead, on the urging of his agent, the legendary Fred Corcoran, played and won at Saint Andrews in 1946. In 1953, Ben Hogan played in his only Open Championship at Carnoustie. He won in very impressive style, but the travel to and from Britain was very hard on him. He never returned to defend his crown and in fact never competed again. Other than these two U.S. victories, the Claret Jug was passed around by Harry Cotton, Fred Daly, Bobby Locke, Peter Thompson, and finally Gary Player. Although these were great champions, the lack of substantial prize money coupled with the time and expense necessary to travel kept most of the well-known American players from competing.

In 1960, The Centenary Open was held at Saint Andrews. Arnold Palmer, who would emerge as the first golf superstar of the electronic media age, finished second to Australian Kel Nagle. Interest in the Open Championship increased dramatically in the States. It seemed that for nearly two decades, the American fans thought that the world's oldest golf championship was something other than a marquee event.

Palmer made the ultimate statement at Royal Birkdale in 1961. He outdueled the field in Palmer fashion, probably best punctuated by his crushing a shot through a bush to the green on the sixteenth hole, saving a par and holding on for a one-stroke victory. This was a great shot in the arm for the Open Championship. It was raised dramatically on the radar of golf aficionados worldwide.

THE VENUE Royal Birkdale is true artistry. The holes meander through the sand dunes in such a fashion that no two holes can be fully viewed from any given point in the fairway. The mixture of holes is breathtaking. There are no repetitions. The strategy differs from hole to hole. Length is a factor on some holes and not at all on others. The wind is always a major element but the design is so clever that the wind never favors or hinders on any two holes in a row. The hazards are simple, yet elegant. The sand hills covered with the ever-present natural grasses are devastating to the wayward player. It

THE SHORT BUNKERS ON NUMBER 5 ARE A STRONG
DETERRENT FOR ATTEMPTING TO DRIVE THE GREEN.

is not unlikely that a ball be lost in the undergrowth, even in the presence of a large Championship crowd. There are 113 bunkers on the course. All of the bunkers are strategic, either blocking an entrance or guarding a target. In many instances the player must play over a hazard, as the circumstance of playing around the trap is more onerous. The bunkers, like most in the British Isles, are unabashedly penal. The penalty can run from half a stroke to a full stroke in the case of some of the fairway pits. The greenside bunkers, unlike their cousins in the States do not provide a bailout for the player. Up and down from a greenside trap is an accomplishment.

THE FIFTH HOLE There are eighteen very good holes at Birkdale. Each is distinctive and laden with the possibilities of disaster. I have chosen the fifth hole for this book.

Number five is a short (344 yards) par four that doglegs left to right from the tee. The green cannot be seen from the tee. For that matter a good deal of the fairway is also not in view.

There are a number of strategies that can be employed from the tee. A three or four iron to the center of the fairway will leave the average touring professional no more than 135–140 yards from the green. A shot 135 from the center of the fairway if well judged will produce a realistic attempt for birdie. A push, a pull, or any shot hit long or short will cause consternation.

Another route is to play a three wood or drive over the right corner of the dogleg and draw the ball back into the fairway. The ball better draw, if not, the player will find the deep craggy rough or

even worse a hidden water hazard. Properly executed, this will leave the average player with no more than a sand wedge or lob wedge to the dance floor.

An especially long accurate driver of the ball could consider going for the green. The drive would need to be about 320 yards to the front apron. The presence of three bunkers left, right, and center, just short of the green sternly discourage this play.

A tee shot that finds the fairway offers the player a chance. The green is visible and inviting although seven bunkers stand sentinel in its surrounds. Any of these bunkers are acceptable by comparison to the prospect of overshooting the green. There is no room beyond the carpet. A large rambling gorse bush and heavily grassed mounds beyond the putting surface will almost certainly spell bogey or worse. The short bunkers and the bunkers to the left of the green are also bad choices for a resting place for the second shot. The short bunkers leave anywhere from 20–40 yards of uncertainty between the player and the green. Nearly every touring professional will tell you that the hardest shot in golf is a bunker play of this ilk. The

ABOVE: THE CLUBHOUSE AT ROYAL BIRKDALE, AN ART DECO MASTERPIECE.

left bunkers are equally difficult in that the green runs away from the player. The right bunker is at a lower point and not as terrifying as its brothers.

Hit the second shot on the green. No problem, except the green is about 3,500 square feet and has a four-foot rise in it. In zeroing in on getting the ball on the proper level, the player must flirt with one body of sand or another. If the player finds the wrong level, three putts becomes a definite possibility. In other words, only two perfectly judged shots will produce birdie or par.

At 344 yards this hole really sounds easy.

THE AILSA
COURSE TURNBERRY NUMBER 6

PULLING OR HOOKING THE TEE SHOT ON THIS
ONE-SHOTTER WILL FIND THE PLAYER IN ONE OF
THESE BUNKERS.

"[Turnberry] is at its best when the crowds have gone and
the evening sun is reflected on land and sea. There is nowhere lovelier."
Donald Steel

TURNBERRY, ENGLAND • 1946
222 YARDS • PAR 3

ONE OF THE MOST memorable days in my golfing life was a wonderfully mild day in Scotland in June of 1987. I was traveling with a group from the Yale Golf Club. We awoke at the Old Course Hotel in Saint Andrews about 6:00 A.M. and showered, dressed, and ate a very quick breakfast. As we awoke, I looked out the window of my room and saw the very first group of the day playing the Old Course. After breakfast we scurried to our rental cars and beat a path to Carnoustie across the Fourth Bridge. Our group of sixteen played in four foursomes and met in the old Clubhouse for lunch. In that we did not have any further golf plans for the day four of us decided to play another round at Carnoustie and meet up with the rest of the group later at the Turnberry Hotel. The four of us that remained subjected ourselves to a second flagellation by the Carnoustie Links and wearily climbed into our

rental and literally tore across Scotland. We pulled into the Turnberry Hotel at the latter part of dusk and when I looked out the window of my room I could just about make out the final foursome of the day leaving the eighteenth green. I considered this quite a feat, seeing three Open venues in one day, playing Carnoustie twice and surviving a two-hour trip across a country that takes three hours to cross. After the best room service dinner I have ever eaten I retired for the evening.

I awoke early the next morning groggy and disoriented. The previous days travel had taken its toll. I looked out the window and shuddered. I was staring at the Ailsa Craig, a mushroom-like stone island that seemingly rises out of the sea. In my partially addled and disoriented mind I thought for a moment the world was coming to an end.

That day was the only time I ever played the Ailsa Course at Turnberry. The Ailsa Course is one of the great rarities in golf. Having only played the course that once, some fourteen years ago, I

remember every hole, nearly every inch of the ground. There are not very many golf courses that are so distinct and so special that I can remember their every turn after such a long time. Merion is Philadelphia and Crystal Downs in Frankfort, Michigan are the only other two that have made that great an impression on me.

The Ailsa Course is a links course in the sense that nine holes are played in one direction and the other nine in the opposite direction. In this case the first eleven go one way with the exception of numbers 1 and 3. At the twelfth tee the player turns back into the wind and has a whole different kettle of fish to deal with. Turnberry is on the West Coast of Scotland hard on the Firth of Clyde. The wind is brisk and biting. Playing the ball down wind from the elevated tees at Turnberry it is not uncommon to see a middle handicapped player drive the ball in excess of 300 yards. Mighty 450-yard par four holes are reduced to a mere three wood from the tee and sand wedge to the green. Everyone is Tiger Woods. Mortality returns on the twelfth tee. The player feels totally abandoned, his great friend and ally has now turned its ugly head and is now the

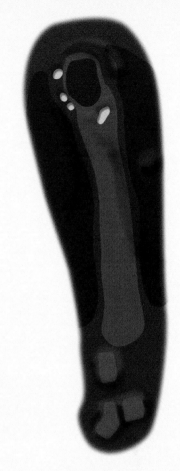

enemy. It is really difficult to stand on the twelfth tee and convince yourself that your swing, which has been fluid and languid for the first eleven holes, will survive in the face of this new adversity. There are a lot of really nasty swings taken on the twelfth tee.

Turnberry offers one of the most majestic grand hotels in the world. The magnificent white structure is on a hill overlooking the two wonderful golf courses. It has been in operation since 1903 and golf has been played on the wonderful

THE GREEN SETTING AND MOUNDS KEEP THE PLAYER IN
TOUCH WITH NATURE AS SEEN HERE AT THE SEVENTH
GREEN AT TURNBERRY.

links land since 1899. During World War I, the Royal Air Force requisitioned the hotel and grounds. The golf courses were abandoned and replaced by landing strips. After the war the course was restored with the help of the renowned James Braid. During World War II, the golf course was once again made into runways. After the war, the British government was convinced to pay reparations to the hotel owners and the Ailsa Course, as we know it today, was designed by Mackenzie Ross.

TAPPIE TOORIE This is the official name of the sixth at Turnberry. I have not the vaguest idea what Tappie Toorie means but I have a feeling that it is Erse for triple bogey.

Number 6 is a 231-yard par three. It plays slightly downhill from the tee and then ever so gently from right to left back uphill to the green. There is a bunker short of the green on the left side that discourages aggressive play. If the player does not carry the bunker from the tee, par is out of the question. At 231 yards club selection is crucial. Any ball that is hit too far will find a rear bunker or the scrub and undergrowth that protects the back of the green. This means the player must hit enough club to reach the dance floor yet not too much as to exceed it. The prevailing wind is at the players back and the green is rather generous.

The best play from the tee is a lofted wood or long iron aimed at the right front and slughtly-drawn toward the target. Par is a very good score here, bogey does not give back much to the field.

THESE DEADLY BUNKERS FRAME THE SIXTH GREEN.

GOLF ON THE
AYRSHIRE COAST ROYAL TROON

"Tam Arte Quam Marte" ("As Much by Skill as by Strength")
Motto of the Royal Troon

NUMBER

7

TROON, ENGLAND • 1878

402 YARDS • PAR 4

IT APPEARED ON THE ROTA IN 1923 as Troon. In that year this fine seaside golf course was the setting for a major upset. Walter Hagen, the defending champion was defeated by one stroke by English Professional Arthur Havers. Apparently, Troon passed the test as a Championship venue. The Open has returned six times.

This is not a great surprise given the list of accomplished architects that graced this ground at one time or another. Willie Fernie laid out the course in the 1880s and Alistar MacKenzie, James Braid, and Frank Pennick further tweaked the links land.

Troon is set on the Ayrshire coast just a few miles north of Turnberry. The Arran Island and Ailsa Craig can be viewed from the course. The course itself has a Jekyl and Hyde personality. It eases out

LOOKING BACK FROM THE GREEN ONE CAN SEE WHY
THIS 402-YARD PAR FOUR IS SO DIFFICULT.

on the front side with two fives, two threes, and five fours. The par five holes at one time would have been considered quite long, but in this day and age 557- and 577-yard par fives are somewhat run of the mill. The longest par four on the front is 423 yards and three of the par four holes are less than forty yards. The incoming nine is an altogether different story. The two par threes are 179 and 223 yards, the one par five measures 542 yards. The par four holes are 438, 463, 431, 465, 457, and 452. Altogether this adds up to a crushing 3,650 yards and par is 35. Only the strong straight drivers of the ball have any chance of success on this monstrous nine.

Troon has produced some marquee name winners. In 1950, Bobby Locke won his second in a row on his way to becoming a five-time champion. Arnold Palmer defended here successfully in 1962 blowing away the competition by six strokes. Tom Weiskopf, who possessed one of the most powerful and graceful swings the game has ever seen, won his only major championship here in 1973. Tom Watson won at Royal Troon in 1983, the Royal having been added in 1978, the one hundredth year of the club's founding. This was Watson's fourth of five victories. In 1989, Mark Calcavecchia bested two Australians, LEFT: ROYAL TROON HOLE NUMBER 7 Wayne Grady and Greg Norman, in a playoff to have his name engraved on the Jug. Justin Leonard played steady and conservative golf and putted unbelievably in taking the crown in 1997.

Probably the best-known hole on the Royal Troon golf course is number eight. Originally known as "Ailsa," this 126-yard demonic little par three is now called the "Postage Stamp." It is a truly simple looking hole that is no more than a small wedge shot for the average touring professional. The green is not very big and is exceptionally well guarded by bunkers on either side. The bunkers will invariably cost the player a shot. Any ball that is hit over the green will cause nothing but trouble. It is not uncommon to watch one group after another make three pars on this hole and then see some unfortunate soul hit the ball in one of the bunkers or over the green and make a six or seven. Gene Sarazen at the age of seventy-one showed the world that this hole is not that difficult. He simply holed out from the tee for a hole in one.

The granite clubhouse at the Royal Troon Golf Club is one of the most elegant of those to be found in the Open rota. It exudes the class and distinction that the player will later find on the course itself. The club secretary Jan Chandler is a living extension of the high-class standards Royal Troon represents.

Royal Troon is a must-play course for the visiting golfer. One's education in the great classic links courses in the world would be incomplete without a round or two here.

ALTHOUGH APPEARING DOCILE, THIS GREEN IS ABUN-
DANT WITH WOE FOR THE INACCURATE APPROACH.

TEL-E-KABIR This hole was chosen on the recommendation of the above-mentioned Mr. Chandler. I feel it is quite a good choice in that it is a hole that can be played successfully by nearly every caliber of player. It measures 402 yards from the championship tee and doglegs every so slightly from left to right from the tee.

The optimum tee shot is played long and down the left side of the fairway avoiding two rather unsavory bunkers that are respectively 283 and 263 yards from the tee. Any ball hit left of these bunkers will probably not be found in the ample accumulation of gorse. From the left side of the fairway, the second shot sets up well.

The angle from the right side of the fairway is not as good and there are two bunkers on the right at almost the same distance from the tee as the ones on the left. To complicate things further, from the right side there are two mounds, just in the rough, that will block the player's view of the green.

The second shot here is critical. The only safe miss is short left of the green. Short right will find a nasty little pot bunker. Right of the green is a nightmarish mix of bunker and gorse. The left side of the green offers another bunker and a mound that will inure that the player will not get close to the pin.

The green is fairly generous but hard to read. Any second shot that fails to get within twenty-five feet will probably lead to bogey.

THE WIND AND THE BUNKERS PLAY HAVOC ON THE APPROACH.

COMFORT AT
HOYLAKE ROYAL LIVERPOOL

THE GREEN THAT TOOK BOBBY JONES SIX TO MASTER IN
HIS FAMOUS VICTORY OF 1939.

"The eighth hole at Hoylake was of some 480 yards, but I had been consistently either on, or just off, the green in two shots. This time was no exception. After a good drive my spoon second just missed the left edge of the green and rolled off some ten or fifteen yards down an innocent slope. It lay still in the fairway with absolutely nothing between it and the flag." Bobby Jones, on his play in the Open championship in 1930

HOYLAKE, ENGLAND • 1869
519 YARDS • PAR 5

WHEN YOU CROSS THE Mersey from Liverpool, whether by ferry or tunnel, you wend your way south and west to a point that juts slightly into the Irish Sea. That point is Hoylake, a small but very distinguished suburb of Liverpool.

When one looks out over the links at the Royal Liverpool Golf Club, little is seen. The linksland, especially around the clubhouse, is just plain dead flat. The first fairway is in plain view as is the eighteenth green and the rock walls that surround the practice area. The whins and the gorse obscure pretty much everything else. This is ingenious deception. After turning the dogleg on the first hole, the land begins to rise and fall ever so gently, yet ever so deceptively, that even the best trained eye can be deceived as to distances. It is this type of subtlety that pervades the entire experience.

Hoylake is ever so subtle, ever so magnificent.

The clubhouse at Royal Liverpool is impressive, yet not foreboding. The interior is well appointed, very classy, and yet comfortable. It is easy to see that the members of this club are comfortable with the surroundings and even more comfortable with their course.

The course was built in 1869 and finished in 1871 making it one of the oldest courses on the West Coast of England. The Open Championship found its way there first in 1897. The course had hosted the first Amateur Championship in 1885 and was at the time the home course of two of the most famous amateur players that have come from the British Isles, Harold Hilton and John Ball. Fittingly, the champion in 1897 was the renowned Harold Hilton. This was Hilton's second Championship, as he had won in 1892 at Muirfield by three shots over John Ball. Ball was the Open Champion at Prestwick in 1890. This was a mere footnote in the career of this great competitor. John Ball between the years of 1888 and 1912 won the Amateur Championship a total of eight times.

In 1902, Sandy Herd at the suggestion of

his friend John Ball used the new Haskell wound ball and won the Open at Liverpool. His employment of the new ball sealed the fate of the old gutta percha ball. If Herd could beat Vardon, Braid, and Taylor there had to be some magic, as the Triumvirate ruled the game at the time.

In all, there were ten Opens contested at Liverpool. None was more famed than the 1930 Open Championship. In late May, Robert Tyre Jones Jr. won his first and only British Amateur crown at Saint Andrews defeating Roger Wethered, 7 and 6 in the final. This was one of the few years that would allow the great Jones the opportunity to attempt to win all four Major Championships. The scheduling of the four major events allowed for attendance and travel. He moved on from Saint Andrews to Hoylake and bested the field there by two strokes, thereby completing the second leg of the Grand Slam. He later returned to the States where he won the U. S. Open at Interlachen and the U. S. Amateur at Merion. This completed the Impregnable Quadrilateral, a feat that will most probably never be equaled in golf. The Modern Grand Slam of the Masters, the U.S. Open, the British Open, and the PGA Championship would be a feat somewhat comparable, yet the debate need not

ALTHOUGH APPEARING DOCILE, THIS GREEN IS
ABUNDANT WITH WOE FOR THE INACCURATE APPROACH.

begin as no man has ever accomplished it in one year.

FAR Far is a pretty simple name for a par five. This hole plays north to south on the eastern edge of the property. The yardage on the hole is 492. In preparation for a possible future Open Championship, the hole could be stretched to nearly 600 yards.

The sight from the tee is wonderful. There is a large fairway bordered by out of bounds to the left and general gunch to the right. Any ball hit out of the fairway will require a skilled second shot to put the player in position to play his third to the green. The fairway is somewhat of a hollow. When one leaves the tee, the ground lowers nearly imperceptibly to a low point on the right side of the short grass. A mound rises beyond the low point obscuring the sight from there to the green.

The aggressive line is the left side of the fairway. A well-struck drive will kick and run on this flatter surface. If one is taking the aggressive line, he flirts ever more with the out of bounds. A good drive will move the player into a position to take a shot at the green in two. Care must still be taken with the second shot even from the optimum position. The out of bounds left

LEFT: ANOTHER VIEW OF THE CLUBHOUSE

continues the length of the hole, but moves further left as the player approaches the green. The area that is created by the absence of the out of bounds is really difficult rough. If the player comes up short and left, he has created his own personal hell. The shot will be undoubtedly from a bad lie in the heavy grass. This is not horrible unto itself but the out of bounds extends a mere few feet over the raised green.

In the 1930 Open final round, Bobby Jones made his way just short of the green in two. When he walked off the putting surface with a triple bogey eight, he just shook his head. The green needs no more explanation than that.

WAR ON THE FIRTH
OF CLYDE TURNBERRY

NUMBER
9

"The ninth and tenth are the embodiment of what lovers of links golf cherish, but they possess more than just scenic value. Again, solid striking is so essential that two 4s are highly valued whatever the conditions." Donald Steel

NUMBER

9

AYRSHIRE, ENGLAND • 1946
454 YARDS • PAR 4

THE FIRST OPEN CHAMPIONSHIP held at the Ailsa Course at Turnberry in 1977 provided as much dram and excitement as any major tournament played in the past three decades. It is not unusual in a Masters, a United States Open, a PGA Championship, or an Open Championship to watch the leaders falter in the final two days of play. There are ample examples of this that do not need to be rehashed. It is often grueling for the golf enthusiast to watch one of his idols eat his liver on the final day. Too many times we have seen brilliant play turn to rank amateur hacking as the prize nears. But every once in a great while. . . .

In 1977, the two best golfers in the world were Jack Nicklaus and Tom Watson. Nicklaus had already won a slew of Major Championships, including three U.S. Opens, five Masters, four PGA

Championships, and two Open titles, at Muifield in 1966 and Saint Andrews in 1970. At 37 years of age Jack was considered the best in the world, perhaps the best that had ever been. Tom Watson, a decade younger, was no less feared by his fellow competitors. He had won the U.S. Open at Pebble Beach by two shots over Nicklaus in 1972 and had his name engraved on the Claret Jug at

THE NINTH TEE AND THE FAMOUS LIGHTHOUSE OF TURNBERRY

Carnoustie in 1975 after beating Jack Newton in a playoff. Jack Nicklaus was one shot away from that playoff in 1975.

After two rounds of the Open Championship in 1977 Nicklaus and Watson were tied with Lee Trevino and Hubert Green, one shot behind leader Roger Maltbie. As luck would have it they were paired together for the third round in the second to last group. They played like men possessed, trading birdie after birdie. When the dust settled at the end of the day both men had shot five under par 65's. The rest of the field at this point was a distant memory.

Sunday was a glorious Scottish day. The sun was shining brightly as the competitors took to the first tee. In quick order Nicklaus took charge over the younger Watson. After four holes Jack held a three shot lead and most golf enthusiasts would have bet their condo in Pinehurst that Watson was done for the day. Jack Nicklaus never beat himself, he never choked, and it had not yet come to pass

that an upstart could spot him three shots with fourteen to play and catch the Master.

Apparently, no one told this to Tom Watson. Nicklaus continued to play steady golf for the next ten holes, but Tom played brilliantly. When Watson holed a 50-plus foot putt from off the green on the par three 15th for birdie, the twosome were once again tied. Both players parred the 16th. On 17, a par five, Watson birdied and Jack missed a short curvy five-foot putt to match him. It was now on to the 18th. Watson smashed a one iron down the left center of the fairway. Nicklaus in an attempt to cut the dogleg and give himself a shorter shot to the green pulled out his driver. He came off the shot and his ball settled in the right rough nestled up to a gorse bush.

Under the intense pressure of the final hole on the final day Watson stroked a magnificent seven iron to within two feet of the hole. Surely the Open was his. But the Golden Bear had other ideas. Somehow he bashed the gorse bush, the Scottish sod, and his golf ball with an eight iron. The ball came to rest on the edge of the green. After long deliberation Jack rolled his ball into the center of the cup for a closing birdie. This seemingly miraculous three made by this giant of the game would have unnerved nearly any player. Watson never flinched, and stroked his ball into the hole.

On the final day the scores read Nicklaus 66 for a total of 269, Watson 65 for the remarkable tally of 268. The next nearest competitor was on 279.

Many epic battles have been fought on the links of the world, but none quite compare with this special mano a mano at Turnberry.

There are eighteen lovely holes at Turnberry. They wander through the dunes right on the beach. From nearly every tee the players can see the Firth of Clyde, the Arran Island, and the Ailsa Craig. The beauty of the course is unmatched anywhere in the world.

The ninth hole at Turnberry mixes the natural beauty of the seaside with a devilishly clever and difficult hole. The hole is located on the highest dune right next to the beach. It is a drop of some eighty feet from the left rough to the beach. For added effect there is a prominent cairn in the middle of the fairway and off to the far left the wonderful 19th century lighthouse that has served as the club's logo since the beginning.

The hole is a 454-yard par four that plays pretty much straight away. There are two things that enter the mind of the player on the tee: Don't hook the ball and don't fade the ball. Neither the right nor the left rough will provide proper egress to the green. This is easily said but not easily accomplished. To have a realistic attempt to reach the green in two the ball must be hit at least 270 yards. This means that the driver will come out of the bag and the big swing will have to be employed.

RIGHT: TURNBERRY HOLE NUMBER 9

So standing on the tee, you let out that last cleansing breath and let it go.

THE ELEGANT LIGHTHOUSE HAS GRACED THE
COAST SOME 150 YEARS.

THE HONOURABLE COMPANY OF
EDINBURGH GOLFERS MUIRFIELD

NUMBER
10

THE SUN SETTING ON THE SEVENTH FAIRWAY
AT MUIRFIELD

"Muirfield has a special place in my heart as I won my first
Open there. It is a demanding driving golf course, yet overall a fair
test of championship-calibre golf." Gary Player

NUMBER

10

MUIRFIELD, GULLANE, ENGLAND • 1891
475 YARDS • PAR 4

AS ONE LEAVES THE pretty little town of Gullane on the East Lothian peninsula toward North Berwick, a street, seemingly an alley, runs from the main road toward the sea. As one slowly drives down the alley, there are signs that the visitor is not welcome to proceed unless that visitor has an appointed reason to be there. On the right, there is the wonderful Greybars Hotel, then a series of garages, and at the dead end, a very impressive gate. Beyond that gate lies the third home of the Honourable Company of Edinburgh Golfers, the vaunted Muirfield. The gate is imposing and forbidding; on the other side is a fairly large gentleman who examines with steely eye all of those who pass through the door in the gate. Those who have trespassed will be turned abruptly to the door.

It is no wonder that this property is gated and guarded. This is a very private club with a set of

rules that go back centuries. The people at Muirfield are not unfriendly, only protective of the grounds and their privacy.

Muirfield is a Mecca for all serious golfers that make their way to Scotland. But Muirfield is also a very busy club that caters first to its members, as it should be. To play Muirfield, one must make arrangements in advance. Too many times this is not done, hence the gate.

A DAY AT MUIRFIELD A day at Muirfield is a one-of-a-kind experience. The member or visitor starts his morning by driving to the club and sequestering his car in one of the garages. He is dressed in jacket and tie knowing that any dress less informal will be greeted by a rebuff at the door. He leaves his clubs with the caddiemaster, who will immediately assign them to one of the many skilled and able caddies. Then he retires to the sparse but sufficient locker room, removes his coat and tie, and puts on his golf toga and shoes and returns to take a few putts on the putting green. Before he leaves the clubhouse the visitor will be greeted or summoned by the

BELOW: THE THIRD GREEN AT MUIRFIELD IS CONSIDERED THE BEST GREEN IN SCOTLAND.

secretary, who will explain the rules and procedures at Muirfield. They are pretty much the same rules and procedures followed at most clubs. At Muirfield, though, they are followed to the letter. There is a good deal of emphasis on the proper speed of play and the courtesies that the visitor is expected to show to the other visitors, the members, and the golf course. All of this is done in cheerful, yet serious, fashion.

After playing the eighteen wonderful holes on the links, the player returns to the locker room to retrieve his jacket and tie. He washes up and prepares for lunch. After passing a cursory inspection at the door to the dining room, he is treated to what is considered to be the best buffet lunch in the Kingdom of Golf. After cocktails and lunch, the members partake in the ritual downing of a strange liqueur known as Kummel.

Fortified with the lunch and a number of quaffs of the elixir, the member reattaches his golf clothes and returns to the links for a game of Foursomes. In this game, there are four players and only two balls in play. A game that is virtually unknown in the States, Foursomes is popular at many of the British and Scottish courses. After the second round is complete, the player will usually retire to a Scotch or gin and tonic, pay his bets, and recount his victories and deficiencies and return home. All in all, not a bad day.

THE CHAMPIONS OF MUIRFIELD The inaugural Open Championship at Muirfield in 1892 was won by

THE ROUGH AND THE BUNKERS CONSPIRE TO
RUIN THE SCORE.

English Amateur Harold Hilton of Hoylake. He was three strokes clear of his fellow club member John Ball, Sandy Herd who was to win at Hoylake in 1902, and defending Champion Hugh Kirkaldy, a native of Saint Andrews.

Harry Vardon won in 1896. James Braid won in 1901 and again in 1906. Ted Ray took the crown in 1912. It was seventeen years before the Open returned to Muirfield. Walter Hagen, the defending champion won the last of his four championships that year. Englishman Alf Perry triumphed in 1935 besting the field by four shots. In the first post–World War II Open at Muirfield in 1948, Henry Cotton won his last of three championships. Gary Player won his first Open at Muirfield in 1959, Jack Nicklaus his first at Muirfield in 1966. Lee Trevino defended the championship he had won in 1971 with a one-shot victory over Nicklaus at Muirfield in 1972. Tom Watson in 1980 and Nick Faldo in 1987 and again in 1992 round out the winner's table at the home of the Honourable Company of Edinburgh Golfers.

THE TENTH HOLE Muirfield, unlike many of the Open venues, is not straight out and straight back. Rather, it is composed of two loops of nine holes, the first running clockwise, the other counter-clockwise. Both loops return to the clubhouse. This composition leaves the tenth tee directly in front of the clubhouse and under the watchful eye of the secretary.

Number ten is just plain hard. It is 475 yards, a par four, plays slightly uphill, and is sprinkled with eight rather strategic bunkers. The first bunkers are found in the driving area guarding the right side of the fairway. It is absolutely imperative to find the fairway off the tee, as the second shot will be hit with either a long iron or a fairway metal. Success with these clubs from the long and straggly rough is nil. One who has hit the fairway will have a long but makeable shot to the green. Those in the rough face the hardship of the second grouping of bunkers that are a little less than a hundred yards from the green. Entering one of these three demons pretty much assures six or more.

The clear line to the green is down the left side to avoid the two bunkers that are found right of the green. The player must be careful not to take the line too far left or the greenside bunker will come into play. The green, like the other seventeen at Muirfield, is flawless yet treacherous. A par on this hole is an adventure and a victory.

THE ROYAL
AND ANCIENT SAINT ANDREWS

"I could take out of my life everything except
my experiences at Saint Andrews
and I'd still have a rich, full life." Bobby Jones

NUMBER

11

SAINT ANDREWS, ENGLAND • CIRCA 1400
172 YARDS • PAR 3

THERE ARE MANY FAMOUS names associated with Saint Andrews and the Old Course. Going back to before the institution of the Open Championship the most prominent was Allan Robertson, who is considered the first golf professional. He was a club and ball maker, a talented player known for his uncanny running iron shots, and the man who was probably responsible for the use of the greens as double greens at the Old Course. Around that same time there was the Cheape family of Saint Andrews. The Cheape family is most responsible for the preservation and succession of the Old Course. It was owned by a number of the members of that family for about 200 years until it was passed to the Royal and Ancient and later the Saint Andrews Links Trust. There is not only a Mr. Cheape's bunker on the course but also a Mrs. Cheape's.

After Robertson came the Morrises, Old Tom and Young Tom. Between the two of them there were eight championships captured. Strangely enough, none of them were won on the Old Course. Tom Morris, the elder, was largely responsible for the final formation of the Old Course. He delineated the holes as they are seen today and built the eighteenth green. The eighteenth hole is named Tom Morris in his honor.

ABOVE: MARKER ON TEE FOR HOLE #11

The Strath family Andrew, George, and David also made contributions to golf at Saint Andrews. Andrew was the greenkeeper under Tom Morris on the Saint Andrews links. He also won the Open Championship in 1865 at Prestwick at a time when those winning the Open were named either Park or Morris. David, or Davie, Strath became a professional golfer at the age of nineteen. He was the professional/greenskeeper at North Berwick. He was involved in one of the strangest Open outcomes of all time. He had tied Bob Martin at 176 for the 36-hole event in 1876 but had violated a rule of the time by hitting a ball onto the seventeenth green prior to the group preceding him had left the surface. The Royal and Ancient did not resolve the rules violation. Instead, they ordered a playoff for the next day. Davie saw no point in a playoff without a resolution of the protest and did not show up for the playoff. Martin won by default. The third brother, George, was not the competitor that his brothers were. He was, though, a fine clubmaker who plied his trade in Glasgow, at Troon, and later in the United States.

THE BUNKERS ARE FLATTER THAN THEIR
COUSINS IN THE STATES, BUT THEIR DEPTH IS
WHAT CAUSES CALAMITY.

Anderson was another famous name at Saint Andrews. The patriarch, David, or "Old Daw," was the keeper of the green at Saint Andrews in early times and fathered two famous sons. His namesake, David Anderson, founded the famous club and the ball making firm of D. Anderson and Son. Another son, Jamie, won the Open Championship three successive years—1877, 1878, and 1879.

The last family of note was the Kirkaldys, Andrá and Hugh. Andrá was a fine player who finished well in the Open Championship tying Willie Park at Musselburgh in 1889, only to lose in a playoff. Andrá was a well-respected high-profile gentleman of Saint Andrews and was chosen to replace Tom Morris as profession upon his retirement. Hugh was not as well known, but he did win the Open at Saint Andrews in 1891. Unfortunately, he died a few years later at the age of twenty-nine.

HIGH IN Alistar MacKenzie wrote of the eleventh at Saint Andrews in the June 1932 issue of the American Golfer: "The Eden Hole on the Old Course at St. Andrews in Scotland, owes its reputation almost entirely to the superlative excellence of its golfing features. It has a large green, sixty yards wide, but the slopes have such a character that it requires a greater variety of shots and gives to more thrills and excitement than any other hole. The various copies that have been made of this hole lack the severe slopes of the original and, comparatively speaking, are dull and insipid."

These are pretty harsh words from the architect who fashioned the fourth hole at Augusta National after the eleventh at Saint Andrews. I believe that he was correct, though. Some things are not the same when taken out of their original context. High In, or The Eden Hole as it is alternately known, is one of those things. In no other place in the world can you have the Eden Estuary as a backdrop, nor can you approximate the whims or velocity of the winds on the Old Course.

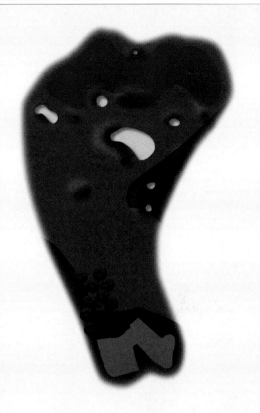

High In is 176 yards of terror. It is utterly do or die. There is one attempt to make the green from the tee and play the hole successfully. There is little or no margin for error. The variables of wind velocity and direction must be calculated accurately. The player must navigate three treacherous bunkers, land on the front of the green, and have his ball stop short of the pin. If he veers too far right or left on the enormous putting surface, he has failed. The break on a thirty-foot putt may be ten to fifteen feet depending on the wind. Any ball struck from above the hole has a very good chance of running directly off the green.

The tee shot can be anywhere from a nine iron to a small wooden club. The player should walk up to his ball and strike it in short order. The longer the player thinks about the Strath bunker, the

ABOVE: SAINT AMDREWS HOLE NUMBER 11

Hill bunker, and the Cockleshell bunker that guard the green, the more doubt will creep into his mind. The eleventh tee is no place to dally.

ELEGANCE AND
GRACE ROYAL SAINT GEORGES

NUMBER
12

THE GREEN AT HOLE #12 WITH THE OUT OF
BOUNDS IN THE DISTANCE

"There is, in the first place, not a single tee shot in the round where
good play must not be shown by the golfer if he wants to achieve success."
Harry Vardon, on playing Royal Saint Georges

NUMBER

12

SANDWICH, ENGLAND • 1887
365 YARDS • PAR 4

IN 1892, the Honourable Company of Edinburgh Golfers moved their facility from the Musselbugh

Golf Links to Muirfield, an adjunct to the town of Gullane, and continued in the rotation of Open

sites with the Royal and Ancient and Prestwick. Two years later it was deemed that other courses

would be showcased and the first in this line was Royal Saint Georges in Sandwich. It was a very good

choice.

The club was established in 1887. In 1885, Dr. Laidlaw Purves and his brother decided to search

for a proper place to build the golf course. Sandwich Bay, where Claudius landed in 43 AD seemed as

good a place as any to begin the search. Sandwich was reachable from London on the rail and the

tower at the St. Clements church was a proper aerie from which to survey the surrounding dunes

land. They did not have to look far.

The land on Sandwich Bay was perfect. It remains that way today. The sandy soil is a magnificent host for the growing of those grasses necessary for a great seaside course. It supports the ever-present bent grass for the playing areas and allows for the flourishing of the seagrass, gorse, and bracken. There is just enough movement in the land to provide for natural elevation changes. The elevation of the dunes accomplishes two purposes. It sequesters one hole from the next, so that each of the eighteen take on the feel of individual theaters. In addition, it reeks havoc in distance calculations that are ever more imperative due to the excessive penalties accessed for misclubbing. A shot hit through the fairway is as likely to be a lost ball as not. A misjudged shot into the greens will put the player either in a bunker or in a position over the green where recovery is at best difficult.

Harry Vardon considered Saint Georges the best course anywhere. He said, "there is, in the first place, not a single tee shot in the round where good play must not be shown by the golfer if he wants to achieve success. The bunkers are so placed that a good shot has to be made every time to carry them. The greens on the course are in all cases well protected, and they abound in LEFT: ROYAL SAINT GEORGES HOLE NUMBER 12 character and variety."

One of the other major assets of the course at Saint Georges is that the holes meander through the dunes. No two holes in a row go in the same direction, so that the wind is not as predicable as other links courses. Saint Georges is very much like Shinnecock Hills in that respect. It is pretty lofty company.

There are eighteen beautiful, strategic, and difficult holes at Royal Saint Georges. The player is required to use his entire arsenal to navigate the links. Navigate is the operative word as there are many areas of the course that no one wants to visit. The rough with the incumbent natural grasses is particularly onerous. Finding a golf ball in this tangled mass of flora, even when the line has been delineated is truly difficult. The longer grass near the fairways grows longer and more intense as one moves farther from the short grass. In addition to the long grass there is no shortage of mounds at Saint Georges. They are frequent and positioned demonically. Just to add a little more chicanery to the mix, there is a liberal sprinkling of bunkers throughout the course. The Marquis de Sade must have placed one bunker on the fourth hole there. It is on the breadth of a mound, has a 45-degree slope, and is actually contained by a wooden surround. If one enters this bunker, he may not emerge.

The last six holes on this course are considered to be as testing as any finish in Open Championship golf. The only respite in this series is the short (163 yard) sixteenth. Thirteen is 443; fourteen, 507; fifteen, 466; seventeen, 425; and eighteen, 468. To play these holes in par or better is a lofty goal. The wind may aid the player on some of them but overall what it gives it takes.

THE GREENSIDE BUNKER IS A MUCH
BETTER OPTION THAN THE BUNKERS SHORT
OF THE GREEN.

NUMBER 12 There has been a good deal written about the long and difficult par four holes at Saint Georges and with good reason. They are back breakers requiring two well-struck and well-paced shots to overcome. The twelfth at Saint Georges does not fall into this category. It is a mere 365 yards, well short of the standards of today, but nonetheless will test the ability of any player.

The hole plays along the dike at the furthest reaches of the property. The tee gives the player no indication of what he faces as there are thirty-foot mounds blocking his view of the hole. The mounds are easily cleared but the placement of the tee shot is crucial. The hole doglegs slightly to the right and there are three bunkers that must be avoided. Distance off the tee is also important, as the player does not want to get too close to the green. Scattered in front of the green are five bunkers that will have to be negotiated on the second shot. This means that the player will have to loft the ball over the bunkers and stop it on the green. A ball that finds its way into a bunker or the rough will present a problem on the second shot. Controlling the distance out of the rough is difficult.

The need for precision that starts at the tee and follows through on the second shot is dictated by the small flat green. This putting surface does not provide any backstop for the player and directly behind the green is a nasty little pot bunker.

This is another prime example of a perfect little par four that depends on deception, placement, and panache to protect par.

THE BACH FUGUES
OF OPEN COURSES   CARNOUSTIE

"The toughest test of golf anywhere in the world."
Gary Player, on Carnoustie after winning the 1968 Open

NUMBER
13

CARNOUSTIE, ENGLAND • 1840S
161 YARDS • PAR 3

THE TOWN OF CARNOUSTIE has spawned numerous sons that have become legends in the lore of golf. Three brothers, Willie, Alex, and MacDonald Smith, hailed from this town on the Firth of Tay. The two lesser-known brothers, Willie and Alex, each won a U. S. Open Crown around the beginning of the 20th century. The better-known MacDonald Smith is probably best known for his flourishing style, which catapulted him toward the top in many national championships. Unfortunately for Mac he never won one.

Stewart Maiden, the legendary club Professional at the East Lake Country Club was a native son of Carnoustie. Maiden is best known as being the mentor of the legendary Robert Tyre Jones Jr. There is little question that the lessons Maiden learned at the stern Carnoustie were related to Jones

THE LADIES GOLF CLUB AT CARNOUSTIE—THE
OLDEST LADIES CLUB IN THE WORLD

CARNOUSTIE LADIES
GOLF CLUB

in rounding out his game.

Carnoustie teaches that nothing in golf is fair. Because of the usual unsavory conditions that are presented at the links, the Carnoustie player learns early that golf is a game of survival. He inures to the situation that a well-struck, well-placed shot sometimes is not enough to overcome the task at hand. Due to the exacting requirements on the Championship course, the Carnoustie player anticipates the hand of fate. A shot that is hit with certainty and skill can often be turned to tragedy by a gust of wind. A slightly misjudged strike often times can result in an out-of-bounds penalty. Many times a player will hit a shot that he feels was perfectly played only to find himself in a lie that cannot be overcome.

Carnoustie more than any other course in the world requires 100 percent concentration. The task at hand must be calculated and then performed. At no other course does the player have to take so much a defensive posture as he does at Carnoustie. If a target cannot be realistically attained there must be a secondary and a tertiary plot. Attacking the golf course is difficult and in most cases foolhardy. One who attacks the links will see all of its teeth. Pure aggression

ABOVE: CARNOUSTIE HOLE NUMBER 13

is repaid with double and triple bogeys. Only the patient, reflective, and uncannily accurate golfer will succeed at Carnoustie.

When the vaunted Ben Hogan came to Carnoustie in 1953, he journeyed by boat. Because of his near fatal accident in 1949 his legs were not strong like those of the average professional player. Even though he was the reigning U. S. Open Champion, as with all the other players, he had to qualify for the Open. He did so on the Burnside Course that abuts the Championship Course at Carnoustie. He was a lead qualifier, yet did not have the time or the strength to play a practice round on the Championship Course. Instead, the day before the tournament Hogan walked the course backward from the eighteenth green to the first tee. He made notes of distances and strategy. He uncovered what he felt were the lines of play necessary to get the task done. He retired to his lodgings and returned the next day for the first round.

The rest is history. The "Wee Ice Man" as the Carnoustie natives took to calling him opened with a 73. He followed with 71, 70, and finished with 68. His legendary ability to concentrate and stick to his game plan carried him to victory. To this day Carnoustie caddies, young and old, can recount each shot he struck in 1953. He played conservative in many places and aggressive where he thought he could. The ultimate thinking man on the course, he will always be considered by those in Carnoustie as the greatest Open Champion.

WHINS The shortest of the three par three holes on the Carnoustie Championship Course, number 13, is still to be respected. Like all one-shot holes the club selection from the tee on this 169-yard jewel is crucial. The player must carry the large bunker that fronts the green, yet not overshoot the target. The green is not very large and heavily contoured. A ball that gets beyond the pin will be cause for a very quick and serpentine putt. A ball that goes beyond the green gives the player a good reason to pick up the ball and head to the fourteenth tee. Par is a good score here, but a well-judged and well-struck tee shot can produce a rare Carnoustie birdie.

IRISH
HUMOR   ROYAL PORTRUSH   NUMBER
14

THE FOURTEENTH GREEN, FROM THE LEFT SIDE,
SHOWING THE DRAMATIC DROP OFF TO THE RIGHT

"Max Faulkner, 1951 Open Champion"
Infamous signature of Max Faulkner's that was signed days previous to his
winning the Open the only time it was held at Royal Portrush

NUMBER

14

PORTRUSH, NORTHERN IRELAND • 1888
210 YARDS • PAR 3

THE NORTHERN COAST OF Northern Ireland is one of the rawest places in the world for weather. Even though the Gulf Stream passes above Ireland to reach the east shore of Scotland, it seems that the temperate climes usually escape Northern Irelands shores. The wind is devastating on a regular basis. No flora in excess of six feet can grow on this coast. Simply the wind will knock it down and carry it away.

On the Northern tip of Northern Ireland lies a bustling little town called Portrush. It is about five miles west of the remains of a medieval fortress known as the Dunluce Castle. The inhabitants of this land, in order to discourage the attacks that were regularly carried out by Scandinavian warriors in the thirteenth and fourteenth centuries, built the castle. Below the grounds of the castle is a

THE TOWN OF PORTRUSH WITH THE VALLEY
COURSE IN THE FOREGROUND.

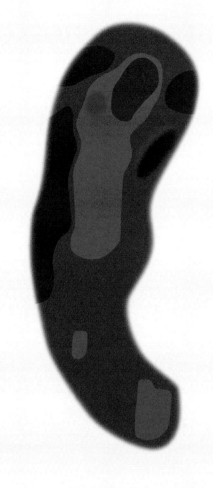

marvelous geological phenomenon known as the Giants' Causeway. The "Causeway" consists of rounded and flat boulders that seemingly grow out of the sea. They are piled one upon another in columns, each a near replica of the next. The local lore speculates that the Causeway was a bridge built by Finn McCool to bridge the channel between Ireland and Scotland, so that the giants could pass over it.

The dunes land in this area of the world is second to none. Magnificent dunes rise one hundred feet or more from the sea. On this dunes land the Royal Portrush Golf Club stands. The original course has a heritage that is somewhat a mystery. The course that is played today is a redesign of the original by Harry Colt. When one looks at the course from nearly any fairway, tee, or green, the first thought is that the course was always there, Harry Colt just knew where to cut the grass.

Like its neighbor to the east, the Royal County Down, Royal Portrush is a perennial member of the top ten courses in the British Isles. Certainly the course has all the attributes to put it in the top ten in the world.

The Open Championship was held here only once in 1951. Englishman Max Faulkner, much to the silent and vocal consternation of the Irish, won it.

The flow of the course at Portrush is as natural as one will find on any course in the world. The holes weave in and out of the dunes in such a manner that one would suspect divine direction. The first hole follows the Dunluce Road away from the clubhouse and the next four holes hug the road to the east. At number five, the course heads directly north to the sea. The backdrop of the North Atlantic behind the fifth green is absolutely breathtaking. From here the course wanders inland and seaward, up and down hill in a manner that presents no real pattern. The wind, which is the predominant hazard, is never the same on two holes in a row. If two successive holes appear to go in the same direction there is just enough bend in one or both to allow the player to truly gauge the breeze. The wind, at least to my many experiences, is not a prevailing wind. Some days it comes from the east, some days from the west, and on the worst of days it barrels in from the sea to the north.

The wind is an ever-curious factor on the two closing holes on this gem of a course. Number 17 heads directly to the west and at 520 yards is a par 5. Number 18, conversely, heads back in the opposite direction. Eighteen is 476 yards long and plays as a par four. If the wind is coming from the east, number 17 can be easily reached with a good drive and a mid-iron. With the eastern wind, putting for eagle is common for even the average player. Getting to the dance floor in two on number 18 in this wind is a feat only accomplished by the finest of players. In an opposite wind, eighteen is easily reachable in regulation but number 17 bares its teeth. There is a bunker about 170 yards off the sev-

enteenth tee. It is well to the right of the fairway but it is truly frightening. About four stories high and built into a 45-degree slope this bunker will catch the drives of those who fade the ball into the wind. Lucky for the player, this bunker is a mere 150 yards from the clubhouse. It is not uncommon to see the visiting golfer find his way from tee to bunker and bunker to bar.

CALAMITY All of the holes at Portrush are worthy of mention. Individually they could each teach a seminar on Golf Course Architecture. Collectively they fit each other like a knight and chain mail. One of the more difficult short par four holes is number 13, the Skerries. It plays up a major dune from one of the lowest points on the course some 380 yards. The green, perched at the end and well guarded by bunkers, is at the northern tip of the course, just about where the dune drops off to the sea. Behind and to the left of the green is the tee for number 14.

The views from the fourteenth tee to the east toward the dune line, to the north toward the sea and to the west toward the Valley course are wonderful. It is only when the player turns his attention to the south where the fourteenth green can be found does terror strike the heart.

At 206 yards, number 14 is what would be considered in this day and age a medium-sized par three. What makes this hole so different is the ground it occupies. The player has his back to the sea when addressing his tee shot. He is looking slightly uphill at a partially obscured green. To the left there is nothing but grief, whins, gorse-covered moguls, and certain ruination. To the right of the narrow fairway is a drop off of monumental proportion. It is straight down approximately 150 feet through thigh-high grass to the bottom of the hill. There is only one avenue, straight up the hill. This is easily written, but with a two iron in your hand and reasonable peripheral vision, even the bravest golfer feels a tug in his chest.

This hole is all or nothing, win or lose. There is little room between par and a dreaded other. The name of the hole is Calamity. Only the Irish would name it that.

HOYLAKE
REVISITED ROYAL LIVERPOOL

NUMBER
15

"[Royal Liverpool's] misfortune is that, in the modern world,
it can no longer accommodate there daily and whose
demands are so consuming in terms of space." Donald Steel

HOYLAKE, ENGLAND • 1869
459 YARDS • PAR 4

ROYAL LIVERPOOL HOSTED ten Open Championships during a seventy-year period beginning in 1897. It was the platform for the most eclectic and international group of champions of any of the Open venues. Two amateurs, Englishman and club member Harold Hilton won the first Open held at his home course; American icon Bobby Jones won in 1930. Scotsman Sandy Herd, using the new Haskell ball, triumphed in 1902. The only Frenchman to win the Open, Arnaud Massy, won in 1907. English Professional J.H. Taylor bested the field in 1913 by eight shots, mostly because of his ability to keep the ball in play in windy and rainy conditions. American professional Walter Hagen won his second Open Championship at Hoylake in 1924. Alf Padgham of Sussex in England took the crown in 1936, beating a field that included Henry Cotton in his prime. In 1947, Irishman Fred Daly from Belfast had his name engraved on the Claret Jug by sneaking past American Amateur Frank Stranahan by one shot. In 1956, Australian great Peter Thompson won his third consecutive Open at Liverpool. Roberto de Vincenzo the only South American to win the Open Championship triumphed at Royal Liverpool.

The club has not been awarded another Open since 1967. There are a couple of reasons for this. Until recently, the club was lacking in practice facilities. To cure this problem, they purchased an adjacent property that provided all of the facility they need. Secondly, it has been thought that the course lacked the length and difficulty to test the players. Roberto de Vincenzo posted a score of 278, 10 under par, in 1967 on the then 6,995-yard layout. This was rather low for the time but is pretty much in line with the scoring that the Open Championship has seen in the past two decades. Nonetheless, Donald Steel, probably the best respected of the native Golf Architects of the British Isles, has lengthened the course by 170 yards recently.

It is not that Liverpool was ever one of the easiest golf courses to play. The opening hole is a terror. It may only play 427 yards, but the out of bounds to the right on this hole that bends 90 degrees to the right is formidable. The prevailing wind is most often in the face of the player and any ball that is faded will disappear into the practice range. The four par 3 holes on this course are as varied and interesting as any in the British Isles. The back nine of the course at the new yardage of 3,648 is as challenging as any Open venue. Steel added some fifty yards to the already difficult seventeenth and

GREEN AND GREENSIDE BUNKERS THAT HAVE CAUSED
SO MANY BIG NUMBERS

about twenty yards to the eighteenth. In addition, he built two new greens for the finishing hole, making them more difficult than in the past.

These improvements along with the great tradition that Royal Liverpool has always portrayed should be sufficient impetus to bring the Championship south across the River Mersey to the shores of the River Dee. Hoylake has been a great part of the Open Championship in the past and should be as significant a part in the future.

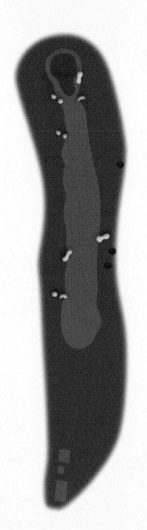

LAKE "Far and Sure" is the motto of the Royal Liverpool Golf Club. Nowhere on this vaunted layout is the idea of far and sure more apropos as it is on the fifteenth hole. This is the beginning of the finish at Hoylake, a 459-yard par four that is followed by a 558-yard par five and two par fours of 449 yards and 416 yards. This is the sternest test of the three.

The hole plays from east to west, nearly assuring a wind that will not favor the player. Most of the time the breeze will cross the fairway from left to right and slightly in the face of the player. The fairway is not terribly generous at about twenty-six yards wide. The drive must be hit down left side

LEFT: ROYAL LIVERPOOL HOLE NUMBER 15

avoiding a short bunker some 220 yards from the tee and another some 260 yards away. A third bunker guards the right side of the fairway at the 285 yard mark. For the professional player of today, this is eminently reachable.

From a comfortable spot in the fairway, about 185 yards from the green, the fun begins. There are two bunkers on the left side of the fairway about fifty yards short of the green. These are effective for gathering balls hit from the rough. The green itself is festooned with four ominous little bunkers, two left and short, one short right, and the final greenside right. If the player can maneuver his ball between these nasty little potholes, he will have a chance at birdie. If not bogey is on the horizon.

FAR FROM
QUIRKY ROYAL LYTHAM & SAINT ANNES NUMBER 16

THIS GREEN WILL GIVE UP SOME BIRDIES, YET THE
BUNKER WILL CAUSE BOGEY.

"It has beautiful turf, but not much else of beauty.
It is a beast but just a beast." Bernard Darwin

NUMBER
16

SOUTHPORT, ENGLAND • 1886
357 YARDS • PAR 4

THE 2001 OPEN CHAMPIONSHIP was held at Royal Lytham and Saint Annes on the Lancashire Coast a stones throw away from the British Coney Island, Blackpool. Over and over the announcers for the television broadcast referred to Lytham as quirky. This proves that there is not only a need for new material for these golf commentators, but also, a general need for new broadcasters.

I imagine that the two reasons they considered Lytham quirky are: a) it is not located right on the water, it is at least three blocks away, and b) Lytham starts with a par three. Unusual, yes, but I have played at least five golf courses that begin with par three holes. All of these courses are at least 75 years old. They were invariably designed by architects limited to the use of the natural land in creating the course. The earth-moving equipment of that age were men and oxen, shovels and Purina Oxen

THE COMFORTABLE, ELEGANT CLUBHOUSE AT LYTHAM
AND SAINT ANNES WITH THE CLOSING HOLE IN THE
FOREGROUND

Chow. The land could not be shaped radically and therefore the occasional short hole starter appeared. Modern day thinking on golf course architecture is that the formula should be a par four or five opener, a mix of four three's, four five's and ten four's. Not a bad formula; boring, unimaginative, but certainly not quirky.

I would describe Royal Lytham and Saint Annes as no less than elegant. The Clubhouse is of classic design, warm and functional. The "Dormie House," which stands behind the first tee and is used to house and feed members and their guests, is a treasure. There is no more convenient or enjoyable way in which to visit a golf club than to stay right on the property. The first tee is well positioned because the chef can come out as you tee off and ask whether you want salmon or lamb for dinner.

The very first Open Championship held at Lytham is the stuff of which legends are made. It was 1926 and Bobby Jones was in the British Isles for the tournaments of note that year. He lost at Muirfield in the fifth round in the Amateur Championship that year and then was victorious in the Walker Cup. In his qualifying rounds at Saint Andrews, he shot 66 and 68.

In the Championship proper Jones was playing head to head with American Professional Al Watrous. Tied on the seventeenth tee on the final day, Watrous placed his drive in the fairway. Jones was slightly wayward finding a bunker on the left side of the fairway 170 yards from the green. Watrous struck a fine shot from the fairway safely on the green. Undoubtedly, he like most of the spectators considered Jones to be cooked. Jones took the modern day equivalent of an eight iron and struck the ball squarely. The ball flew over the gorse and whins and landed on the green inside Watrous' ball. This was more than the befuddled Watrous could handle. He three putted and bogeyed number eighteen. Robert Tyre Jones Jr., the greatest Amateur Golfer of all time, finished with two pars and won his first of three Open Championships.

Nine other competitions for the Claret Jug have been held at Royal Lytham and Saint Annes. Bobby Locke, Peter Thompson, and Gary Player won there. The only left-handed winner of a major event, Bob Charles of New Zealand won at Lytham in 1963. Englishman Tony Jacklin ended a seventeen-year streak of foreign winners in the Open by taking the crown in 1969. In 1979, 22-year-old Seve Ballesteros jumped to the front page of the world golfing news by hitting the ball everywhere but on the fairway and winning the Jug. He was the youngest winner of the 20th century. Ballesteros returned in 1988 to win again.

The last two winners at Royal Lytham and Saint Annes were Tom Lehman in 1996 and David Duval in 2001. Certainly these two names add nothing but additional honor to the already storied tradition at Lytham and Saint Annes.

So to those who say quirky, I say rubbish!!!

NUMBER 16 Number 16 at Lytham and Saint Annes is a respite hole. It is sandwiched between two monster par four holes, number 15 at 463 yards and number 17 at 469 yards. Although it looks easy on paper this is really the last good chance for birdie on the golf course.

To play this hole effectively, the player must position a three wood in the left side of the fairway around 240 yards from the tee. In doing this he must avoid the three bunkers that are in the left rough. If he pushes his drive to the right side of the fairway or worse the right rough, the angle to the green diminishes. In playing linksland golf the angle of approach is crucial. Because the wind, either at one's back or in one's face, is so strong it is much more desirous to get the ball on the ground as soon as possible. The longer it is in the air, the greater effect the wind will have. If playing into a heady wind a wedge shot that will go 125 yards normally might only cover 90-95 yards. This is the difference between playing a third shot from the rough or one of the many bunkers surrounding the green and putting from five or six feet. The same is true of the wedge going downwind. If the ball flies too far the left side bunkers and as well as the gorse bushes and scrub behind the green are now in play.

From the left side of the fairway the player has a straight path to all corners of the green. He can elect to "knock down" a short iron, keeping it from being affected greatly by the wind and run the ball to the hole. The sixteenth green at Lytham, like the other seventeen, is well conditioned and true. If the player has been smart and accurate, he should have little problem converting a short birdie putt.

FROM THE GREEN LOOKING BACKWARD, THIS HOLE
SEEMS SIMPLE.

WHERE CADDIES ARE
A NECESSITY PRESTWICK NUMBER 17

"Though uncertainty is the salt of the game, such a
degree of uncertainty as this is not conducive to bringing to a fine
test relative golfing merit." Horace Hutchinson

NUMBER

17

PRESTWICK, ENGLAND • 1851
391 YARDS • PAR 4

PRESTWICK NEEDS MORE explanation than was given in the first chapter. For the player traveling to Prestwick the first time, I would heartily recommend the employment of one of the local caddies. There are a few reasons for this: first, Prestwick has some fairly good elevation changes and carrying your bag up and down can be a chore. Secondly, the caddies are really friendly and cheerful, qualities that might allay some of the utter frustration of the game. Most importantly, the caddies know where the holes are.

When you leave the second green, the third tee is not terribly hard to find. When you stand on the tee, the hole is difficult to find. All you can see is a relatively wide fairway, which comes to an abrupt end at the beginning of a large bunker. Logically, you hit your shot down the middle of the

THE ENORMOUS SHORT BUNKER GUARDING THE
SEVENTEENTH GREEN.

short grass and walk out after it. Once you have arrived at the ball you would have to be Carnac to figure out what is next. If you guess straight away, you have probably seen the last of that Titleist. After the bunker the hole actually bends nearly 90 degrees and the green is somewhere far away hidden by a mogul strewn fairway. The fifth hole is a wonderful par 3 known as The Himalayas. The tee is right behind the fourth green but where it goes from there is a bit of a puzzle. The only clue is a target that is on a pole on the top of an adjacent hill. One group that a doctor friend of mine played with had no difficulty figuring out the avenue of play; after all, they were all professional men. There was major consternation, however, when three of the four hit the target dead on. None of the three balls were found.

The Himalayas is followed by a series of five of the finest par 4 holes to be found in all of Scotland. They are all straightforward and difficult. Because of the way in which they were laid out at least two of them will be played directly into the wind. Since three of these are in excess of 430 yards, the player is assured to have a long way home at least twice. Even on mild days in Prestwick, the wind is at least two clubs. Many times the wind can be the equivalent of four clubs. For players from the States who are used to milder breezes, the idea of a hard seven iron from ninety yards is foreign. At Prestwick, it is an integral part of the game.

Starting on the fifteenth tee, the caddie again becomes a necessity. Although the player can see a good part of the fifteenth hole from the tee, Sherlock Holmes could not figure out where to hit the

drive. The fairway rises about 125 yards from the tee and that which lies beyond the hill is a true mystery. There are bunkers (including one rather onerous one on the right side in the driving area), little hillocks covered with the ever-present seaside grasses and one of the narrowest fairways one could imagine. Number sixteen is a tiny (288-yard) par 4 that one would swear has no fairway at all. At the end of this bunker- and bracken-filled fairway is a mean and guileless green that will test the skill of any purveyor of the flat stick.

The eighteenth is a rather mundane affair: a short (284-yard) par 4, that is mostly straight away. It was the venue of one of the most hilarious events I ever witnessed on a golf course. In 1987, I was playing with a group that had traveled all over Scotland for about a week. As often happens, my partner and I had to win the eighteenth to salvage what had been a fairly bad day. Our opponents had won 16 and 17 and were really feeling their oats when one of the two drove the ball on the front of the green some seven feet from the hole. My partner and I hit, sure that our fate was sealed. After all, our opponent was putting for eagle on this decisive hole. As we ambled down LEFT: PRESTWICK HOLE NUMBER 17 the fairway, the superintendent drove up to the front of the green in his trusty carryall truck. He proceeded to lift the flag and pulled the plastic cup out of the ground. My horrified opponent started racing down the fairway pulling his clubs on a trolley. He was yelling all his might while clubs were bouncing out all over the place. By the time he reached the green, the hole was plugged and he engaged the greenkeeper with some less than courteous chatter, including some speculation as to the lineage of the chap. The superintendent, mostly ignoring this fellows bellows, turned and said "Don't bother me, I have work to do." At this point he drove to the very back of the green and drilled a hole some eighty-five feet from where my opponent's ball sat. Four putts later, my partner and I had recovered some of our pride. I believe our opponent attempted to set a new lager consumption record in the nineteenth hole.

THE ALPS Some great golf holes are created by architects, some by shapers, others by just plain dumb luck. Number 17 at Prestwick was created by nature and discovered by Old Tom Morris. The player has numerous options on the tee of this 391-yard par 4. There are bunkers to navigate, rough to avoid, and position for a second shot to be considered. The aggressive player will take the straight line to a diminishing fairway that ends at the base of a seventy-foot mound. The closer the player comes to the end of the fairway, the more accuracy is necessary. There are reasonably generous landing areas left and right, but they lie further from the eventual target.

To play this hole sensibly from the tee, the player has to look for the stone on the hill to see what

THIS BELL SIGNALS "ALL CLEAR" WHEN LEAVING THE SEVENTEENTH GREEN.

part of the green the pin is located on. If the pin is left, the play is to the left. If the pin is right, then the player must position himself on that side of the fairway.

Choice of clubs on the second shot is crucial. The green is about forty feet from the bottom of the mound and the area from the top of the hill to the front of the green is covered with moguls that in turn are covered with nightmarish undergrowth. In essence, you either hit the green or face certain doom. Long of the green is another exercise in cruelty. The green itself is a classic, somewhat bowl-shaped but with many curious twists and turns. It takes two very well thought-out shots to get to the dance floor and one or two very well placed putts to achieve success.

The Alps is one of the most widely copied holes that lie on Scottish golf courses. It is in the same category as the Road Hole at Saint Andrews and the Redan at North Berwick. Like these fabled holes, the original Alps always outshines the copies.

THE SWEEPING, SLOPING GREEN AT HOLE #17 WITH THE
INCUMBENT HAZARDS IN SIGHT

CLEARING THE
BARRY BURN CARNOUSTIE NUMBER 18

THE EIGHTEENTH GREEN LOOKING BACK OVER THE
BARRY BURN

"I think this is the hardest on the (British Open) rotation.
It's also definitely the fairest because there's only one blind tee shot. . . .
On most links, you don't see everything." Tiger Woods

NUMBER

18

CARNOUSTIE, ENGLAND • 1840S
486 YARDS • PAR 5

THE ONLY NON-BRAND name winner at Carnoustie is a man who has already become somewhat of a footnote in Open legend, although his triumph was in 1999. Paul Lawrie, a Scot from Aberdeen, won a three-way playoff that year over Justin Leonard and the ill-fated Frenchman Jean van de Velde.

Van de Velde, a European Tour player had played magnificently through the first seventy-one holes of the tournament. He had carded 75, 68, and 70 on the first three days of the tournament in conditions that were particularly windy. The weather was not the only unfriendly factor. The course preparation narrowed the fairways and let grow wild the incumbent cabbage surrounding the playing field. So hard was the set-up that the thirty-six hole cut was twelve over par. Van de Velde continued his fine play on Sunday, reaching the eighteenth tee at three over par for the day and three shots clear

THE MADDENING SHORT BUNKERS ON THIS DRACONIAN HOLE.

PLEASE REPAIR BALL MARKS

of the field. All the Frenchman needed was a double bogey six to gain the coveted prize.

To set the stage, the eighteenth needs explanation. It is a man-sized 495-yard par four. Normally played at 444 yards, it was deemed that the best in the world should have to add another fifty or so yards to further test their mettle. The fairway is fairly wide although not so far from the left of the fairway is an out of bounds hazard. This lurks in the backs of the minds of the players forcing them to think right. Right is good, but not too far right. The Barry Burn runs down the far right of the fairway offering no forgiveness. Closer to the fairway are three pot bunkers that are just in the rough. These three bunkers are of the variety that allows the player to think that egress with a suitable club to reach the green is possible. Many of the world's greatest golfers have been fooled by these demonic hazards and make what they think are perfect swings, only to find the ball at their feet when the dust settles. This happened to Johnny Miller in the final round of the 1975 Open Championship. He

chose a six iron from the bunker nearest the green and made what appeared to be a perfect swing. The ball caught the last layer of sod on the revetted bunker and came back to his feet. He managed to get his next shot to the green but failed to sink the putt. He finished third to Tom Watson and Jack Newton by one stroke. Watson beat Newton the next day in a playoff.

There is another major hazard on this hole. The Barry Burn,

which runs down the far right side of the rough, turns and crosses the fairway about twenty yards short of the green. The perfect second shot must clear the Barry Burn. If it does, it will likely find its way to the putting surface. By the way, if the second is hit too hard it will exceed the green and go directly out of bounds.

There are three prime examples of how not to play this hole. This author witnessed one, another was related by a very good friend, and the third was seen by the entire world.

The first comedy of errors began with a slightly errant drive from a seven-handicap friend of mine who was having a good day on the links. He had come to eighteen only four over par, no small feat for any player. He hit the ball well but just a touch too far right. He caught the first of the pot bunkers. He entered the trap with his seven iron and a determined look. Four or five swings later, he emerged chagrined and holding his ball. To prove that the previous day was no fluke, he nearly repeated the performance the next morning. This time he did get out of that bunker, but the five swings he took in the next bunker was causation for the same result.

My good friend Bob Berry related the following to me. Bob is a very good player, well seasoned

and with great panache. That day, he had none of those qualities. Carnoustie had literally eaten his lunch. On eighteen he hit a short crooked drive and followed it with two more foozles. From 120 yards from the green, he once again topped the ball causing it to find a watery grave. Totally flustered, Bob turned to his caddie and said, "I have a mind to jump in that burn and drown myself." The caddie did not miss a beat when he retorted, "I doubt you could keep your head down that long."

The fate of Van de Velde would be as amusing if it had not cost him the Championship. In what appears to have been a major mental lapse, Van de Velde took his driver from the tee. He only had to make six; he could have reached the green with three seven-iron shots. Nonetheless, he pushed his drive badly. The drive was bad but the result was fortunate. His ball came to rest on the other side of the Barry Burn in the seventeenth fairway. From here he could have hit a pitching wedge back to the eighteenth fairway and played another wedge to the green. But apparently this was not the manly way to approach things. He decided to play a two iron from 210 yards to the green from a not terribly good angle. The shot hit the grandstand that had been erected over the far

ABOVE: THE LUNCH HUT AT CARNOUSTIE IS ONE OF THE BEST VALUES ANYWHERE.

right of the burn and caromed off into the high grass short of the burn. His lie was not good; most lies in that type of rough are not. He went straight at it, hit it fat, and found a watery grave. After a good deal of deliberation, Jan decided to drop behind the burn and played his next into the greenside bunker. From there, the ill-fated European Tour veteran made a remarkable up and down for a triple bogey. He tied Paul Lawrie and Justin Leonard but was so rattled that he was no factor in the four-hole playoff. This assured, at least for the twentieth century, that the only French name on the Claret Jug would be Arnaud Massey, who won in 1907.

You might find it curious why I have only related ways not to play the eighteenth hole at Carnoustie. This is because I truly believe that the only way in which to play this monster is under an assumed name.

RIP : PRINCES

THE THIRD COURSE on the Kent Coast that has hosted an Open Championship is the Princes Course. It is adjacent to Royal Saint Georges and the property shares the dunes line that runs up the coast.

Princes only hosted one Championship on its 6,890-yard par 74 course. The course had three par three holes and five par five holes. Gene Sarazen with the aid of a newly invented sand wedge and the council of legendary caddie Skip Daniels bested the field by five shots. This was the only victory in the Open Championship for "The Squire," yet was the only one necessary to complete the lifetime Grand Slam. When Sarazen won the Masters, a half a decade later, he became the first to have won each of the four professional major tournaments.

PRINCES MAY NOT HAVE THE ORIGINAL COURSE,
BUT TODAY'S COURSE IS WELL GROOMED.

MODERN GOLF ARCHITECTURE IS MELDED WITH
THE TRADITIONAL AT PRINCES.

OF COURSE THE ART OF BUNKERING WAS NOT
LOST TO THE NEW DESIGN.

DRAMATIC ELEVATIONS CHANGE ON A RELATIVELY
FLAT GROUND.

While Sarazen went on to bigger and better things, Princes did not fare as well. Once the social capital of the Kent Coast, the worldwide depression eroded its financial base. Just as times were starting to get better, World War II began and the fate of the Princes course was sealed.

As it had been requisitioned during World War I, Princes was once again called upon to be a training ground and staging area for troops during the World War II. Like its neighbor Royal Saint Georges, Princes' property suffered greatly during the war. The course was virtually destroyed. Unlike Saint Georges, Princes did not have the wherewithal to survive and rebuild. The financial base was not sure enough to restore the old course and continue as a private club. So Princes, the Open venue, rests in peace.

But Princes is not forgotten. The elegant clubhouse that overlooks the Channel has been boarded up for many years. It is now scheduled for restoration to be used as housing at the 2003 Open at Saint Georges.

The original eighteen-hole layout has been replaced with three nines. Bill Howie, the Secretary/Manager of Princes and the General Manager of the Bells Hotel in Sandwich assured me that all is well at Princes. Now an accessible quasi-public venue, Princes is by far the busiest of the three courses on the dunes line.

And so it goes. If you have the great fortune to visit the Kent Coast, do not ignore Princes. The old course may be gone but the spirit remains.

2001, DAVID DUVAL, ROYAL LYTHAM AND SAINT ANNES / 2000, TIGER WOODS, SAINT ANDREWS / 1999, PAUL LAWRIE, CARNOUSTIE / 1998, MARK O'MEARA, ROYAL BIRKDALE / 1997, JUSTIN LEONARD, ROYAL TROON / 1996, TOM LEHMAN, ROYAL LYTHAM AND SAINT ANNES / 1995, JOHN DALY, SAINT ANDREWS / 1994, NICK PRICE, TURNBERRY / 1993, GREG NORMAN, ROYAL SAINT GEORGES / 1992, NICK FALDO, MUIRFIELD / 1991, IAN BAKER-FINCH, ROYAL BIRKDALE / 1990, NICK FALDO, SAINT ANDREWS / 1989, MARK CALCAVECCHIA, ROYAL TROON / 1988 SEVE BALLESTEROS, ROYAL LYTHAM AND SAINT ANNES / 1987, NICK FALDO, MUIRFIELD / 1986, GREG NORMAN, TURNBERRY / 1985, SANDY LYLE, ROYAL SAINT GEORGES / 1984, SEVE BALLESTEROS, SAINT ANDREWS / 1983, TOM WATSON, ROYAL BIRKDALE / 1982, TOM WATSON, ROYAL TROON / 1981, BILL ROGERS, ROYAL SAINT GEORGES / 1980, TOM WATSON, MUIRFIELD / 1979, SEVE BALLESTEROS, ROYAL LYTHAM AND SAINT ANNES / 1978, JACK NICKLAUS, SAINT ANDREWS / 1977, TOM WATSON, TURNBERRY / 1976, JOHNNY MILLER, ROYAL BIRKDALE / 1975, TOM WATSON, CARNOUSTIE / 1974, GARY PLAYER, ROYAL LYTHAM AND SAINT ANNES / 1973, TOM WEISKOPF, ROYAL TROON / 1972, LEE TREVINO, MUIRFIELD / 1971, LEE TREVINO, ROYAL BIRKDALE / 1970, JACK NICKLAUS, SAINT ANDREWS / 1969, TONY JACKLIN, ROYAL LYTHAM AND SAINT ANNES / 1968, GARY PLAYER, CARNOUSTIE / 1967, ROBERTO DE VICENZO, ROYAL LIVERPOOL / 1966, JACK NICKLAUS, MUIRFIELD / 1965, PETER THOMSON, ROYAL BIRKDALE / 1964, TONY LEMA, SAINT ANDREWS / 1963, BOB CHARLES, ROYAL LYTHAM AND SAINT ANNES / 1962, ARNOLD PALMER, TROON / 1961, ARNOLD PALMER, ROYAL BIRKDALE / 1960, KEL NAGLE, SAINT ANDREWS / 1959, GARY PLAYER, MUIRFIELD / 1958, PETER THOMSON, ROYAL LYTHAM AND SAINT ANNES / 1957, BOBBY LOCKE, SAINT ANDREWS / 1956, PETER THOMSON, ROYAL LIVERPOOL / 1955, PETER THOMSON, SAINT ANDREWS / 1954, PETER THOMSON, ROYAL BIRKDALE / 1953, BEN HOGAN, CARNOUSTIE / 1952, BOBBY LOCKE, ROYAL LYTHAM AND SAINT ANNES / 1951, MAX FAULKNER, ROYAL PORTRUSH / 1950, BOBBY LOCKE, ROYAL TROON / 1949, BOBBY LOCKE, ROYAL SAINT GEORGES / 1948, HENRY COTTON, MUIRFIELD / 1947, FRED DALY, ROYAL LIVERPOOL / 1946, SAM SNEAD, SAINT ANDREWS / 1945, NO CHAMPIONSHIP / 1944, NO CHAMPIONSHIP / 1943, NO CHAMPIONSHIP / 1942, NO CHAMPIONSHIP / 1941, NO CHAMPIONSHIP / 1940, NO CHAMPIONSHIP / 1939, RICHARD BURTON, SAINT ANDREWS / 1938, REG WHITCOMBE, ROYAL SAINT GEORGES / 1937, HENRY COTTON, CARNOUSTIE / 1936, ALF PADGHAM, ROYAL LIVERPOOL / 1935, ALFRED PERRY, MUIRFIELD / 1934, HENRY COTTON, ROYAL SAINT GEORGES / 1933, DENSMORE SHUTE, SAINT ANDREWS / 1932, GENE SARAZEN, PRINCES / 1931, TOMMY ARMOUR, CARNOUSTIE / 1930, BOBBY JONES, ROYAL LIVERPOOL / 1929, WALTER HAGEN, MUIRFIELD / 1928, WALTER HAGEN, ROYAL SAINT GEORGES / 1927, BOBBY JONES, SAINT ANDREWS / 1926, BOBBY JONES, ROYAL LYTHAM AND SAINT ANNES / 1925, JIM BARNES, PRESTWICK / 1924, WALTER HAGEN, ROYAL LIVERPOOL / 1923, A. G. HAVERS, ROYAL TROON / 1922, WALTER HAGEN, ROYAL SAINT GEORGES / 1921, JOCK HUTCHINSON, SAINT ANDREWS / 1920, GEORGE DUNCAN, ROYAL CINQUE PORTS / 1919, NO CHAMPIONSHIP / 1918, NO CHAMPIONSHIP / 1917, NO CHAMPIONSHIP / 1916, NO CHAMPIONSHIP / 1915, NO CHAMPIONSHIP / 1914, HARRY VARDON, PRESTWICK / 1913, J. H. TAYLOR, ROYAL LIVERPOOL / 1912, EDWARD RAY, MUIRFIELD / 1911, HARRY VARDON, ROYAL SAINT GEORGES / 1910, JAMES BRAID, SAINT ANDREWS / 1909, J. H. TAYLOR, ROYAL CINQUE PORTS / 1908, JAMES BRAID, PRESTWICK / 1907, A. MASSEY, ROYAL LIVERPOOL / 1906, JAMES BRAID, MUIRFIELD / 1905, JAMES BRAID, SAINT ANDREWS / 1904, JACK WHITE, ROYAL SAINT GEORGES / 1903, HARRY VARDON, PRESTWICK / 1902, ALEX HERD, ROYAL LIVERPOOL / 1901, JAMES BRAID, MUIRFIELD / 1900, J. H. TAYLOR, SAINT ANDREWS / 1899, HARRY VARDON, ROYAL SAINT GEORGES / 1898, HARRY VARDON, PRESTWICK / 1897, H. H. HILTON, ROYAL LIVERPOOL / 1896, HARRY VARDON, MUIRFIELD / 1895, J. H. TAYLOR, SAINT ANDREWS / 1894, J. H. TAYLOR, ROYAL SAINT GEORGES / 1893, WILLIE AUCHTERLONIE, PRESTWICK / 1892, H. H. HILTON MUIRFIELD / 1891, HUGH KIRKALDY, SAINT ANDREWS / 1890, JACK BALL JR., PRESTWICK / 1889, WILLIE PARK JR., MUSSELBURGH / 1888, JACK BURNS, SAINT ANDREWS / 1887, WILLIE PARK JR., PRESTWICK / 1886, DAVID BROWN, MUSSELBURGH / 1885, BOB MARTIN, SAINT ANDREWS / 1884, JACK SIMPSON, PRESTWICK / 1883, WILLIE FERNIE, MUSSELBURGH / 1882, BOB FERGUSON, SAINT ANDREWS / 1881, BOB FERGUSON, PRESTWICK / 1880, BOB FERGUSON, MUSSELBURGH / 1879, JAMIE ANDERSON, SAINT ANDREWS / 1878, JAMIE ANDERSON, PRESTWICK / 1877, JAMIE ANDERSON, MUSSELBURGH / 1876, BOB MARTIN, SAINT ANDREWS / 1875, WILLIE PARK, PRESTWICK / 1874, MUNGO PARK, MUSSELBURGH / 1873, TOM KIDD, SAINT ANDREWS / 1872, TOM MORRIS JR., PRESTWICK / 1871, NO CHAMPIONSHIP / 1870, TOM MORRIS JR., PRESTWICK / 1869, TOM MORRIS JR., PRESTWICK / 1868, TOM MORRIS JR., PRESTWICK / 1867, TOM MORRIS SR., PRESTWICK / 1866, WILLIE PARK, PRESTWICK / 1865, ANDREW STRATH, PRESTWICK / 1864, TOM MORRIS SR., PRESTWICK / 1863, WILLIE PARK, PRESTWICK / 1862, TOM MORRIS SR., PRESTWICK / 1861, TOM MORRIS SR., PRESTWICK / 1860, WILLIE PARK, PRESTWICK /

2001, DAVID DUVAL, ROYAL LYTHAM AND SAINT ANNES / 2000, TIGER WOODS, SAINT ANDREWS / 1999, PAUL LAWRIE, CARNOUSTIE / 1998, MARK O'MEARA, ROYAL BIRKDALE / 1997, JUSTIN LEONARD, ROYAL TROON / 1996, TOM LEHMAN, ROYAL LYTHAM AND SAINT ANNES / 1995, JOHN DALY, SAINT ANDREWS / 1994, NICK PRICE, TURNBERRY / 1993, GREG NORMAN, ROYAL SAINT GEORGES / 1992, NICK FALDO, MUIRFIELD / 1991, IAN BAKER-FINCH, ROYAL BIRKDALE / 1990, NICK FALDO, SAINT ANDREWS / 1989, MARK CALCAVECCHIA, ROYAL TROON / 1988 SEVE BALLESTEROS, ROYAL LYTHAM AND SAINT ANNES / 1987, NICK FALDO, MUIRFIELD / 1986, GREG NORMAN, TURNBERRY / 1985, SANDY LYLE, ROYAL SAINT GEORGES / 1984, SEVE

BALLESTEROS; SAINT ANDREWS / 1983, TOM WATSON, ROYAL BIRKDALE / 1982, TOM WATSON, ROYAL TROON / 1981, BILL ROGERS, ROYAL SAINT GEORGES / 1980, TO
JOHNNY MILLER, ROYAL BIRKDALE / 1975, TOM WATSON, CARNOUSTIE / 1974, GARY PLAYER, ROYAL LYTHAM AND SAINT ANNES / 1973, TOM WEISKOPF, ROYAL TROON
/ 1968, GARY PLAYER, CARNOUSTIE / 1967, ROBERTO DE VICENZO, ROYAL LIVERPOOL / 1966, JACK NICKLAUS, MUIRFIELD / 1965, PETER THOMSON, ROYAL BIRKDALE
1960, KEL NAGLE, SAINT ANDREWS / 1959, GARY PLAYER, MUIRFIELD / 1958, PETER THOMSON, ROYAL LYTHAM AND SAINT ANNES / 1957, BOBBY LOCKE, SAINT ANDR
1952, BOBBY LOCKE, ROYAL LYTHAM AND SAINT ANNES / 1951, MAX FAULKNER, ROYAL PORTRUSH / 1950, BOBBY LOCKE, ROYAL TROON / 1949, BOBBY LOCKE, ROYA
CHAMPIONSHIP / 1943, NO CHAMPIONSHIP / 1942, NO CHAMPIONSHIP / 1941, NO CHAMPIONSHIP / 1940, NO CHAMPIONSHIP / 1939, RICHARD BURTON, SAINT ANDREW
HENRY COTTON, ROYAL SAINT GEORGES / 1933, DENSMORE SHUTE, SAINT ANDREWS / 1932, GENE SARAZEN, PRINCES / 1931, TOMMY ARMOUR, CARNOUSTIE / 1930,
JONES, ROYAL LYTHAM AND SAINT ANNES / 1925, JIM BARNES, PRESTWICK / 1924, WALTER HAGEN, ROYAL LIVERPOOL / 1923, A. G. HAVERS, ROYAL TROON / 1922, V
CHAMPIONSHIP / 1917, NO CHAMPIONSHIP / 1916, NO CHAMPIONSHIP / 1915, NO CHAMPIONSHIP / 1914, HARRY VARDON, PRESTWICK / 1913, J. H. TAYLOR, ROYAL LIV
/ 1908, JAMES BRAID, PRESTWICK / 1907, A. MASSEY, ROYAL LIVERPOOL / 1906, JAMES BRAID, MUIRFIELD / 1905, JAMES BRAID, SAINT ANDREWS / 1904, JACK WHITE
/ 1899, HARRY VARDON, ROYAL SAINT GEORGES / 1898, HARRY VARDON, PRESTWICK / 1897, H. H. HILTON, ROYAL LIVERPOOL / 1896, HARRY VARDON, MUIRFIELD /
KIRKALDY, SAINT ANDREWS / 1890, JACK BALL JR., PRESTWICK / 1889, WILLIE PARK JR., MUSSELBURGH / 1888, JACK BURNS, SAINT ANDREWS / 1887, WILLIE PARK
1882, BOB FERGUSON, SAINT ANDREWS / 1881, BOB FERGUSON, PRESTWICK / 1880, BOB FERGUSON, MUSSELBURGH / 1879, JAMIE ANDERSON, SAINT ANDREWS / 18
MUSSELBURGH / 1873, TOM KIDD, SAINT ANDREWS / 1872, TOM MORRIS JR., PRESTWICK / 1871, NO CHAMPIONSHIP / 1870, TOM MORRIS JR., PRESTWICK / 1869, TOM
/ 1864, TOM MORRIS SR., PRESTWICK / 1863, WILLIE PARK, PRESTWICK / 1862, TOM MORRIS SR., PRESTWICK / 1861, TOM MORRIS SR., PRESTWICK / 1860, WILLIE PA
ROYAL BIRKDALE / 1997, JUSTIN LEONARD, ROYAL TROON / 1996, TOM LEHMAN, ROYAL LYTHAM AND SAINT ANNES / 1995, JOHN DALY, SAINT ANDREWS / 1994, NICK
ANDREWS / 1989, MARK CALCAVECCHIA, ROYAL TROON / 1988 SEVE BALLESTEROS, ROYAL LYTHAM AND SAINT ANNES / 1987, NICK FALDO, MUIRFIELD / 1986, GREG N
ROYAL TROON / 1981, BILL ROGERS, ROYAL SAINT GEORGES / 1980, TOM WATSON, MUIRFIELD / 1979, SEVE BALLESTEROS, ROYAL LYTHAM AND SAINT ANNES / 1978, JA
LYTHAM AND SAINT ANNES / 1973, TOM WEISKOPF, ROYAL TROON / 1972, LEE TREVINO, MUIRFIELD / 1971, LEE TREVINO, ROYAL BIRKDALE / 1970, JACK NICKLAUS, S
NICKLAUS, MUIRFIELD / 1965, PETER THOMSON, ROYAL BIRKDALE / 1964, TONY LEMA, SAINT ANDREWS / 1963, BOB CHARLES, ROYAL LYTHAM AND SAINT ANNES / 1962
LYTHAM AND SAINT ANNES / 1957, BOBBY LOCKE, SAINT ANDREWS / 1956, PETER THOMSON, ROYAL LIVERPOOL / 1955, PETER THOMSON, SAINT ANDREWS / 1954, PET
BOBBY LOCKE, ROYAL TROON / 1949, BOBBY LOCKE, ROYAL SAINT GEORGES / 1948, HENRY COTTON, MUIRFIELD / 1947, FRED DALY, ROYAL LIVERPOOL / 1946, SAM S
CHAMPIONSHIP / 1939, RICHARD BURTON, SAINT ANDREWS / 1938, REG WHITCOMBE, ROYAL SAINT GEORGES / 1937, HENRY COTTON, CARNOUSTIE / 1936, ALF PADGHA
PRINCES / 1931, TOMMY ARMOUR, CARNOUSTIE / 1930, BOBBY JONES, ROYAL LIVERPOOL / 1929, WALTER HAGEN, MUIRFIELD / 1928, WALTER HAGEN, ROYAL SAINT (
LIVERPOOL / 1923, A. G. HAVERS, ROYAL TROON / 1922, WALTER HAGEN, ROYAL SAINT GEORGES / 1921, JOCK HUTCHINSON, SAINT ANDREWS / 1920, GEORGE DUNCAN,
VARDON, PRESTWICK / 1913, J. H. TAYLOR, ROYAL LIVERPOOL / 1912, EDWARD RAY, MUIRFIELD / 1911, HARRY VARDON, ROYAL SAINT GEORGES / 1910, JAMES BRAID
1905, JAMES BRAID, SAINT ANDREWS / 1904, JACK WHITE ROYAL SAINT GEORGES / 1903, HARRY VARDON, PRESTWICK / 1902, ALEX HERD, ROYAL LIVERPOOL / 1901,
ROYAL LIVERPOOL / 1896, HARRY VARDON, MUIRFIELD / 1895, J. H. TAYLOR, SAINT ANDREWS / 1894, J. H. TAYLOR, ROYAL SAINT GEORGES / 1893, WILLIE AUCHTERL
1888, JACK BURNS, SAINT ANDREWS / 1887, WILLIE PARK JR., PRESTWICK / 1886, DAVID BROWN, MUSSELBURGH / 1885, BOB MARTIN, SAINT ANDREWS / 1884, J
MUSSELBURGH / 1879, JAMIE ANDERSON, SAINT ANDREWS / 1878, JAMIE ANDERSON, PRESTWICK / 1877, JAMIE ANDERSON, MUSSELBURGH / 1876, BOB MARTIN, SA
CHAMPIONSHIP / 1870, TOM MORRIS JR., PRESTWICK / 1869, TOM MORRIS JR., PRESTWICK / 1868, TOM MORRIS JR., PRESTWICK / 1867, TOM MORRIS SR., PRESTWIC
PRESTWICK / 1861, TOM MORRIS SR., PRESTWICK / 1860, WILLIE PARK, PRESTWICK / 2001, DAVID DUVAL, ROYAL LYTHAM AND SAINT ANNES / 2000, TIGER WOODS, S
AND SAINT ANNES / 1995, JOHN DALY, SAINT ANDREWS / 1994, NICK PRICE, TURNBERRY / 1993, GREG NORMAN, ROYAL SAINT GEORGES / 1992, NICK FALDO, MUIRFIE
AND SAINT ANNES / 1987, NICK FALDO, MUIRFIELD / 1986, GREG NORMAN, TURNBERRY / 1985, SANDY LYLE, ROYAL SAINT GEORGES / 1984, SEVE BALLESTEROS, SAI
1979, SEVE BALLESTEROS, ROYAL LYTHAM AND SAINT ANNES / 1978, JACK NICKLAUS, SAINT ANDREWS / 1977, TOM WATSON, TURNBERRY / 1976, JOHNNY MILLER,
MUIRFIELD / 1971, LEE TREVINO, ROYAL BIRKDALE / 1970, JACK NICKLAUS, SAINT ANDREWS / 1969, TONY JACKLIN, ROYAL LYTHAM AND SAINT ANNES / 1968, GARY
SAINT ANDREWS / 1963, BOB CHARLES, ROYAL LYTHAM AND SAINT ANNES / 1962, ARNOLD PALMER, TROON / 1961, ARNOLD PALMER, ROYAL BIRKDALE / 1960, KEL NA
THOMSON, ROYAL LIVERPOOL / 1955, PETER THOMSON, SAINT ANDREWS / 1954, PETER THOMSON, ROYAL BIRKDALE / 1953, BEN HOGAN, CARNOUSTIE / 1952, BOBBY LO
HENRY COTTON, MUIRFIELD / 1947, FRED DALY, ROYAL LIVERPOOL / 1946, SAM SNEAD, SAINT ANDREWS / 1945, NO CHAMPIONSHIP / 1944, NO CHAMPIONSHIP / 1943